Art in Paper

Also by CARSON I. A. RITCHIE:
   Modern Ivory Carving
   A History of Shell Carving
   Bone and Horn Carving: A Pictorial History

Art in Paper

Carson I. A. Ritchie

South Brunswick and New York:
A. S. Barnes and Company
London: Thomas Yoseloff Ltd

A. S. Barnes and Co., Inc.,
Cranbury, New Jersey 08512

Thomas Yoseloff Ltd
108 New Bond Street
London W1Y OQX, England

Library of Congress Cataloging in Publication Data

Ritchie, Carson I   A
   Art in paper.

   Bibliography: p.
   Includes index.
   1.Paper work.   I. Title.
TT870.R55   745.54'09   74-9296
ISBN 0-498-01489-4

PRINTED IN THE UNITED STATES OF AMERICA

For Eileen

Contents

Introduction

O F all the substances that have become the vehicle for artistic creativity, paper is perhaps the most interesting. Although often credited to a Chinese inventor, Tsai Lun, who is supposed to have developed paper in A.D. 105 as a substitute for what was then the writing material of China, bamboo slips, it is worth stressing that paper is a completely natural substance, invented by Nature herself. Jules Michelet, the nineteenth-century French etymologist, gives a classic exposition of Nature's paper makers, the wasps: "They suspend their edifice in the air, and build it of strong coarse paper to defy the heaviest rains. To make this paper they hasten to the forest, where they select some thoroughly prepared wood, which has been long soaking, and has been already steeped by nature just as we steep flax. Then within, with a strong sharp tooth, they gnaw, and tear, and loosen, and sever the rebellious filaments, pound them into pulp as we do the linen rags, and knead them with a heavy tongue. After the paste has been mixed with a viscous and adhesive saliva, it is spread out into thin layers. With teeth closed like a press, the work is completed. The elementary substance of the paper is prepared."[1]

The actions that the wasp carries out successively—obtaining bark which has been soaked in water, pounding it into a pulp to loosen the fibers, spreading them out in a flat layer, and allowing them to dry—are, of course, the same steps adopted by the Chinese paper maker in making his product. Just because paper is a natural product reproduced by man through following nature's methods, artists have always felt at home with it, just as they have with natural substances like ivory, shell, bone,

---

[1.] Jules Michelet, *The Insect* (London: Nelson and Son, 1875), p. 285.

or horn, and it has repaid this sympathy extended to it by allowing itself to be formed into some of the most cherished treasures of art.

Because paper is not a precious material but one within everyone's grasp, these treasures have not always been appreciated as they ought to have been. It is only in comparatively recent times that we awoke to the discovery that whatever has been touched by the hand of a master retains something of his virtue. Sir Alfred Gilbert, the English sculptor who created London's best known statue, *Eros*, in Picadilly Circus, was a master craftsman in bronze and many colored alloys, but the artistic ability which most impressed his students was the fact that he could make great sculpture just out of the silver paper which had wrapped his tobacco.

It is only in very recent times that we have discovered Chinese and Polish paper cuts, *origami*, and paper sculpture, and rediscovered the silhouette. It is possible that new and undiscovered treasures in paper are still to be found in a re-examination of world art. Unfortunately, many of them have been lost forever. Paper is an ephemeral substance. Just because it is a natural product, it offers an irresistible temptation to many kinds of insects, animals, and birds, either to use it to build their homes, like the wasps, or simply to eat it. The arsenic added to the cardboard masks and figures used in the Chester miracle plays by medieval artists has not prevented these lost masterpieces from being consumed by rats or some other of time's destructive agencies. The very transient nature of paper, however, may have positively encouraged some artists to work in it. A creation undertaken in such a fragile material could be made lightheartedly. This may be one of the reasons why paper has attracted so many women. Paper is a material where the sexes meet on equal terms and a male artist is not benefited by his superior muscular strength; rather, it is a substance where neatness and cleverness are of great advantage. For whatever reason, there can be no doubt that some of the greatest of women artists have made their contribution to world art in paper.

Just because everybody could afford to buy a piece of paper it has always been a favored material for the poor folk artist, such as the wandering Chinese "pilgrim of lakes and rivers." Yet, paradoxically, paper craft seems to have had a strong attraction for the great as well. Queen Anne of England amused herself by cutting paper ships; George III took a great interest in paper art. The poor folk artist, and royalty, are combined in the person of Hannah Robertson, surely one of the most extraordinary women in the history of art, the granddaughter of Charles II, who is compelled to support herself by making rolled paper.

Paper art is important, not just in itself, but because of the inspiration it provided for artists in different fields. Symmetrical paper patterns formed the blueprints for Renaissance ironwork, for Chinese porcelain designs, and for Japanese lacquerwork. The paper shape has been a perpetual inspiration to architects, from the Bauhaus school back to medieval Egypt. Speaking of the mosque of Ibn Tulun, in Cairo, Egypt, with its spiral facade, Robert Curzon remarks: "The minaret belonging to this magnificent building has a stone staircase winding round it out-side: the reason of its having been built in this curious form is said to be that the vizier of Sultan Tayloon found the king one day lolling on his divan and twisting a piece of paper in a spiral form; the vizier re-marking upon the trivial nature of the employment of so great a mon-arch, he replied, 'I was thinking that a minaret in this form would have a good effect: give orders, therefore that such a one be added to the mosque which I am building.' "

A substance so universal in its scope that it can either be snipped into an art form on the inspiration of a moment, form the life's work of a great professional artist, or be fashioned according to the traditional tenets of a school of folk art which has taken centuries to emerge cannot fail to find an echo, in one of its protean forms, in all my readers' hearts.

Art in Paper

1

Chinese Funerary Paper

*T*HE idea of paper funeral decorations is not exclusively Chinese. In Abbott's Ann, Dorset, England, a maiden's garland or memorial chaplet, consisting of a gilt paper crown decorated with paper rosettes, was carried before the coffin to the grave at the funeral of a young, unmarried person. Five white paper gloves were attached to the garlands, representing a challenge thrown down to any person who would dare to asperse the character of the dead. In the Middle Ages, a gauntlet thrown on the ground was the sign of defiance. If someone picked the gauntlet up, it meant that he was prepared to fight. If no one picked up the paper gauntlets, they were hung up, with the crowns, in the church, as a proof of the purity of the deceased. Many crowns still hang in an Abbott's Ann church, near to the west end. The oldest of them dates back to 1716.

Although paper decorations at funerals may have been used in other parts of Europe, no mention of them seems to have survived. In China, however, paper is inseparable from funerals, and anyone who thinks about funerals must think about paper, in the same way that Mao Tse Tung, writing a poem on July 1, 1958, about the extirpation of schistosomiasis in the Yangtze Valley, says that he is prepared to offer the god of plagues a paper boat, so that he can make a speedier journey to the next world.

The use of paper tomb figures, funerary paper money, and the like, in old China, which seems to us in the West so superstitious, had its roots in the sound common sense of the Chinese people. In Europe,

graves were dug over and tombs re-used unless the families who claimed
them exercised the greatest vigilance. In China, all that a family had to
do to "stake a claim" to its ancestral tombs was to scatter paper money
round them, and tie some of it to the stones of the ancestors' resting
place at the Feast of Tombs. Anyone who then violated such a main-
tained grave would face the full rigors of the Chinese legal code respect-
ing disturbing the dead.

The Chinese use of paper tomb figures and the burning of paper
money at the funeral goes back very much further than the first lengthy
account we have of this practice, which is given by that observant
traveler, Marco Polo, in 1287. In his account of a funeral in Tangut, a
province of Tartary which bordered on the western part of China, he
told his readers: "Another ceremony also is practised on these occasions.
They provide a number of pieces of paper, made of the bark of a certain
tree, upon which are painted the figures of men, women, horses, camels,
pieces of money, and dresses, and these they burn along with the corpse,
under the persuasion that in the next world the deceased will enjoy the
services and use of the domestics, cattle, and all the articles depicted
on the paper."[1]

During the rule of the Han dynasty (206 B.C.-A.D. 25), real money,
not paper replicas of cash, had been placed in the tombs of the dead.
Even at this early date, however, tomb robbers were just as active in
China as they were in 1928, when thieves despoiled the tomb of China's
last empress, Tzu Hsi. Emperor Wu Ti (140-86 B.C.) had the mortifi-
cation of learning that his ancestral tombs had been robbed. A less
tempting substitute for the real thing had to be found, and very shortly
after its invention by Tsai Lun, paper was used to make imitation coins,
covered with gold or silver foil, to place in the tombs instead of real
ones. Perhaps the use of this paper tomb money, which began to be
regularly buried with the dead during the reign of the Emperor Ho Ti
(A.D. 89-106) may have suggested the first issue of authentic paper cur-
rency, during the reign of the Emperor Kao Tsung (A.D. 650-683), who
lived during the Tang Dynasty.

It was a small step from converting coins into imitation paper money
deposited with the dead to turning the real sacrifice of costly materials,
such as silk, made at the funeral, into an imitation sacrifice. In the reign
of the Emperor K'ai Yuan (A.D. 713-739), Wang Yu, the Master of
Ceremonies, began to burn paper tomb money at the Imperial Sacrifices.
Contemporary scholars protested. They felt—and they were right in this
assumption—that this practice would be copied by ordinary folk. Some

[1] *The Travels of Marco Polo* (London: Heron Books, No date), p. 105.

of the apprehension felt by scholars of the time was justified. Most Chinese paper used to be made from bark, and the constant consumption of paper at funerals helped to convert the "Flowery Land" into a country where there are a great many more rocks than flowers, and where the forests which were once extensive enough to harbor elephants and rhinos have now almost wholly disappeared.

Though the sacrificial paper money used at funerals was probably printed, it must have been pin-pricked as well, because during the reign of Hui Tsung (A.D. 1101-26)of the Sung Dynasty, two ministers of the crown petitioned the Emperor to complain of the custom of burning "perforated paper made to resemble money." The great American historian of paper, Dard Hunter, inferred from these words that the paper was made up in the shape of coins, with holes by which it could be strung, just like real copper cash. There is a belief in parts of China, however, that if you pierce a piece of paper with many minute perforations, and then sacrifice it by setting it on fire, any demon who happens to be about at the time will be forced to jump through each pinhole before the fire reaches it, thus completely losing face.

The custom of burning paper images of objects that would in former times be sacrificed to the dead, either by breaking them or burning them, or that represent live creatures, such as wives or horses intended to accompany their masters on their long journeys, is probably as old as paper itself. Though Marco Polo speaks only of painted images on paper, not sculptured figures, he is, after all, describing what took place in an outlying province of Kublai Khan's great empire, not China itself.

It seems reasonable to assume then, that the Chinese had early evolved most of the paper crafts we know today: paper sculpture, represented by the funeral images; paper cutting, exemplified in the paper money and paper cuts burned as a sacrifice to the spirits; paper money, which would have to be cut by hand, because the embossing machine was not yet invented; pin-prick work, because some of this paper was perforated; and collage, because some of it was coated with gold and silver metal foil. Paper work had thus become an occupation for both the professional and the amateur. In China, and wherever the Chinese had penetrated, special craftsmen labored to construct meticulously made paper sculptures of objects which were destined to be burned at the dead man's bier, and serve him in the next world. Young girls, such as the Boat People of Hong Kong today, also made paper grave goods, as part of their trousseaus.

To the Chinese, paper was a sacred material, associated with religion as well as funerals. Special ornamental incinerators were to be found in temple courtyards, to the left of the main buildings. There, on days of sacrifice, paper images and "spirit" paper would be burned. Bundles of bamboo and straw spirit money could be seen piled up on the ground under the eaves of country temples, all ready to go up in flames as a sacrificial offering. The color of the paper, white, was the color of mourning in China, but it was also the color of immorality. Paper ribbons were tied to the willow trees planted on tombs, emblematic of belief in the new life of the world to come.

Not everyone could afford a sculptured image, but everyone could, and did, buy paper deities, the picture of a god printed or painted on a slip of paper, or just the god's name written out in characters. The kitchen god and the gate god were to be found, portrayed in paper, in every Chinese home, from the Emperor's Palace to the lowest hovel.

In the old-fashioned Chinese "Paper Shop," which will be described in a moment, the pictures of hundreds of different deities could be bought. These representations of gods, known as the "Chih Ma," or "paper horses," are burned at the New Year Festival to honor the "Hundred Deities." The term "paper horses," is a reminder of the time when, before the Tang Dynasty, real horses and people, had been sacrificed at the funerals of important personages, not just paper images. When the First Emperor was buried in 210 B.C. for example, his son said: "It is not fitting that the concubines of my late father who are without children should leave him now."[2] So the concubines, and the workmen who had constructed the tomb, perished as sacrifices.

By the nineteenth century, when Europeans begin to leave us accounts of their work, the image makers of funerary paper worked in open-fronted shops among the narrow streets and courts of the city. The facades of their shops were decorated with gaily painted mirrors, while inside their wares could be seen hanging. These included Mandarin coats made entirely from paper and gorgeously painted in the correct ceremonial embroidery styles, replica strongboxes with silver paper locks, hats, shoes, and other clothes. The paper workers made full-sized carts and horses, as well as sedan chairs, servants, and furniture. By the twentieth century motor cars and radios had been added to their repertoires. Many of the objects they made looked so realistic that when one traveler in China brought back with him a paper radio, the customs official who cleared his baggage refused to believe that it was not a real one until he had lifted it up and found how light it was. One of the best selling lines of the image maker was his horses—which will be

---

[2.] Herbert A. Giles, *The Civilisation of China* (London: Williams and Norgate, 1911), p. 31.

Seventeenth or early eighteenth-century portrait of a lady. COURTESY BRITISH MUSEUM. PHOTOGRAPH BY STELLA MAYES REED.

Paper cut of a vase of flowers, possibly seventeenth century. Flowers have always been a favorite subject with paper artists. COURTESY BRITISH MUSEUM. PHOTOGRAPH BY STELLA MAYES REED.

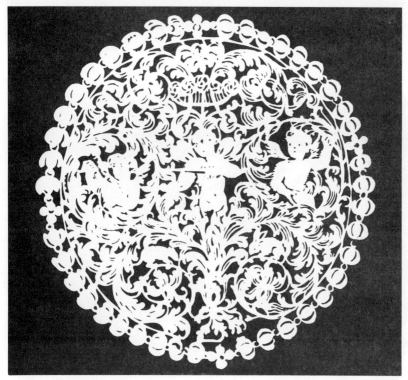

This delightful locket paper cut may be from the seventeenth century. Cherubs and heraldic devices figure largely in paper cuts of this period. COURTESY BRITISH MUSEUM. PHOTOGRAPH STELLA MAYES REED.

The ship was a favorite device for paper artists, such as the eighteenth-century master who created this paper cut. COURTESY BRITISH MUSEUM. PHOTOGRAPH BY STELLA MAYES REED.

Eighteenth-century English paper cut of Neptune and seahorses. COURTESY BRITISH MUSEUM. PHOTOGRAPH BY STELLA MAYES REED.

This little eighteenth-century English paper cut of an owl was intended to be mounted in a glass-fronted locket or pendant—a form of paper jewelry, once common, which ought to be revived. COURTESY BRITISH MUSEUM. PHOTOGRAPH BY STELLA MAYES REED.

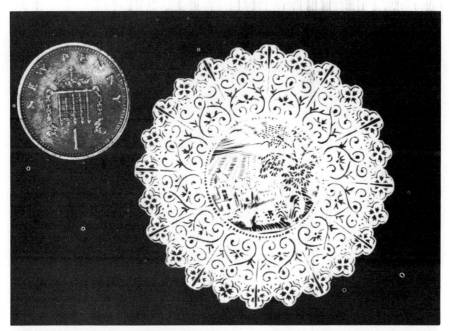

It is difficult to tell whether this charming English paper cut of the eighteenth century is the work of a folk artist or a professional. COURTESY BRITISH MUSEUM. PHOTOGRAPH BY STELLA MAYES REED.

described in a moment—and his sedan chairs. The moment any Chinese died his relatives burned a paper sedan chair and two coolies to help his spirit on its way. Paper boats were also burned. The custom of rendering respect to the dead man's spirit the instant he had died often produced disastrous fires within the home as the relatives burned the paper offerings. The larger paper images, which will be described later, were burned outside.

Though there appears to be no direct evidence to point to this fact, it seems safe to assume that the image makers also made the gold and silver spirit money known as *kwan tiao*. At the beginning of the twentieth century this changed hands at the rate of $100 spirit money for $4 silver. Spirit money could be bought at the "paper shop," which, in places like Hong Kong, where the Chinese have not been forced to alter their traditional way of life and death, still offers a wide variety of goods to its customers. At a paper shop you can buy not merely paper images, or pictures, of all the gods, but complete sets of new clothes for them. Nothing makes mortals happier than a new outfit, and in China the gods are made in man's image. In Hong Kong the local deity, Tam Kung, is

An eighteenth-century English paper cut, possibly deriving inspiration from lace patterns. COURTESY BRITISH MUSEUM. PHOTOGRAPH BY STELLA MAYES REED.

presented with an official hat in the style of the Chou Dynasty, together with ceremonial robes and riding boots. The White Monkey, another deity, is given a gold paper crown, red jacket, imperial yellow cloak, and white shoes for hopping from cloud to cloud. Paper models of buildings, such as the Moon Palace, burned in Kiangsu, on the Festival of the Measure, are also on sale, but the most popular item is undoubtedly paper money. This consists of ingots covered with gold or silver paper, dollars covered with tin foil, and banknotes often marked, in modern Hong Kong, "Hell Bank Note."

A few bold spirits had protested against this enormous consumption of paper and metal. An official of the Emperor Chen Tsung (A.D. 998-1023) of the Sung Dynasty exclaimed as he lay on his deathbed, and noticed his family already beginning to burn paper offerings: "How can the spirits be intelligent, and yet accept bribes?" General opinion was on the other side, however, and the King of the Nether World and his attendant courtiers and bureaucrats were looked on as a rather venal lot, not above accepting a *douceur*.

A few years before the end of the Chinese Empire, in 1904, Lady Susan Townley, the wife of a British diplomat in Peking, described for us the use of paper funeral images at Peking funerals. One funeral which she attended was that of a shopkeeper: "I saw a kind of altar, probably the domestic shrine of the deceased, in whose shop the funeral service was taking place, on which stood burning incense and paper offerings arranged around a Buddha. . . . At the back of the shop was a table, on which were arranged in rows of three, at least a dozen horses about two feet high. They were made of the same paper as that employed for Chinese lanterns, and were grotesquely coloured to represent the quadruped. Being jointed at the neck and tail they moved gently as the wind came in at the door. All these horses were burnt when the dead man was finally carried from his house to be buried, his spirit being supposed to ascend with the rising smoke.

"It was a curious procession which started from the door. . . . The coffin was covered with a scarlet cloth embroidered with gold, and on the top of it was fixed an immense paper stork made after the same

An eighteenth-century paper cut of the Lord's Prayer, framed in an open-work border of flowers, made in England by a professional paper artist.
COURTESY BRITISH MUSEUM. PHOTOGRAPH BY STELLA MAYES REED.

Eighteenth-century English paper cut of an owl. COURTESY BRITISH MUSEUM.
PHOTOGRAPH BY STELLA MAYES REED.

Portrait of Jonathan Swift by an unknown English (or possibly Irish) paper cutter. The slashes outline what would be the black lines in the engraving. Note how small complete composition is. COURTESY BRITISH MUSEUM. PHOTOGRAPH BY STELLA MAYES REED.

Eighteenth-century French canivet, *illustrating a fable.* COURTESY BRITISH
MUSEUM. PHOTOGRAPH BY STELLA MAYES REED.

fashion as the horses, and coloured like them to represent the real bird,
but looking even more grotesque than they did as it swayed this way
and that on its long thin legs, its wagging head keeping time with its
nods to the steps of the bearers."[3]

Another funeral which Lady Susan Townley witnessed, at which
paper images figured largely, was that of the eminent Chinese statesman,
Li Hung Chang: "In the courtyard of the house of mourning were

[3.] Lady Susan Townley, *My Chinese Note Book* (London: Methuen), p. 200-202.

arrayed a whole menagerie of weird beasts over lifesize, their coats and plumage being represented by dried fir twigs. I noticed an immense and most comically-shaped Chinese pug amongst others. There was also a small regiment of life-sized horses, constructed on light bamboo frames covered with paper and coloured to imitate life. Each one was mounted by a Chinaman in correct official dress, with hat, boots, and pig-tail complete. These stuffed cavaliers in their coloured paper garments looked so lifelike as almost to deceive one at a short distance. Looked at closely, however, it was impossible not to laugh at the fixed expressions of man and beast; the cavaliers sat their horses so primly, and all looked in the same direction with such a sweet smile on their painted faces. The comic side of the whole thing was still further accentuated when presently man and beast were bodily hoisted up and carried away on men's shoulders to the place of their execution, for all were burnt in the evening in order that the deceased statesman might have the use of them in the spirit world to which he was supposed to have retired. In the same way were sent after him the effigies of his servants, houses, Peking carts, family shrines, official chairs, and wives."[4]

On the following morning Lady Susan saw a second procession: "Of paper horsemen, animals, carriages, and servants, similar to those burnt on the previous night, carried aloft on mens' shoulders,"[5] as the old statesman's funeral cortege passed through the streets of Peking.

The framework of the paper images was made up of thin strips of bamboo, which were covered with many thicknesses of paper, and finally painted in water colors. The image makers were highly skilled professionals who would turn out competent portraits of men or animals. Dard Hunter saw them laboring on the likeness of a favorite mastiff, which was to be burned at its master's funeral. Paper craft never became a professional specialty in China, however. The traditional paper work of the Boat People of Hong Kong has already been referred to. The bride of a boatman brings with her a box of funeral clothes, which she has made herself, and which are destined to be burned at her husband's ancestral shrine.

4. Ibid., p. 247.
5. Ibid.

2
Origami

MOST lovers of art probably feel that *origami* paper folding is an art confined to Japan, and that it is the most artistic type of paper folding in Japan. Both these views need some modification. In China, no less than Japan, paper folding is a very ancient art, and in America and Britain paper folding was an essential part of life much more than in the Far East. During the nineteenth century, for example, the working man, on both sides of the Atlantic, rarely appeared without his folded paper cap. Every child of the Anglo Saxon race who played at soldiers wore a triangular cap of folded paper imitating that worn by generals and admirals, and when, outside of play hours, he dared to throw a paper dart in class, he did punishment in the corner of the room, wearing a conical-shaped hat of folded paper, which has given us the name for our largest size of writing paper today—"foolscap." Once released from detention, he forgot his sorrows by making a paper boat from the foolscap and sailing it in the gutter on his way home from school. *Origami* is an art created for the amusement of children, but has ended up by delighting millions of grownup people.

The first Japanese paper was imported from Korea around 610. As an imported material, it early acquired the glamor of an expensive, exotic material, one of the treasures which came from the mysterious continent of Asia and which has given the name *maru* (treasure) to all Japanese ships of today. From a foreign import, paper became transformed into a home-grown product of the highest excellence. Japanese paper was made from the tough and pliant inner bark of several species

The occasion of forging a sword, wrote A. B. Mitford, is "invested with a certain sanctity, a tasseled cord of straw, such as is hung before the shrines of the Kami, or native god of Japan, being suspended between two bamboo poles in the forge, which for the nonce, is converted into an altar." Nineteenth-century Japanese print. PHOTOGRAPH BY STELLA MAYES REED.

The paper folded wands in the corners of this box wrestling ring are five-colored, symbolizing the Five Grains and giving a religious importance to Japan's national sport. Nineteenth-century Japanese woodcut. PHOTOGRAPH BY STELLA MAYES REED.

A WRESTLING MATCH.

Champion wrestler wearing rope girdle with paper foldings emphasizing the sacred nature of wrestling. Nineteenth-century Japanese woodcut. PHOTOGRAPH BY STELLA MAYES REED.

of trees, including the mulberry, the *Mitsumata* and the *gampi*. These trees have a bark which contains long, tough, fiber cells. The stripped-off bark is not hacked and cut to bits, as in Europe, but lovingly pounded by hand in a mortar, so that the long cells are softened and separated, but not severed, consequently the tensile strength of their fibers is transferred, whole, to the paper into which they are made. If a piece of hand-made Japanese paper is held up to the light, a glance will reveal the fibers running through it in all directions, an almost invisible network which holds the whole page together. The earliest European technologist to examine Japanese paper, the German savant, J. J. Rein, remarked: "Japanese bark paper evinces a surprising toughness and flexibility, and combines the softness of silk paper and the firmness of a woven texture."

Nowhere else but in Japan could such a variety of fine papers be obtained. Even early Chinese visitors to Japan, who never seem to have anything favorable to say about the country which had done so much to reproduce the best in Chinese civilization, had to praise Japanese colored paper.

Paper made from *gampi* was sold in thin, light, transparent sheets. It could be crushed, folded, and rolled into a ball, then straightened out without suffering any damage.

These qualities were essential for the development of *origami*, and modern experts who have re-created old *origaimi* designs described in ancient text books have stressed that these designs can only be made in strong, flexible, hard wearing paper. Just as Japan invented the folding fan, which needs tough, flexible paper, so it created *origami* out of the most suitable raw material for it that could have been devised, *gampi* paper.

An incredible range of textures and colors awaited the purchaser. Red, blue, indigo, yellow, and green papers were used in Japan as early as the Nara period. By Heian times, men and women courtiers mortified themselves by pulping their old love letters into a greyish, speckled paper, on which they then copied the sutras in ink made with silver or gold dust. Crepe papers were made from old Kozo papers, which had been remade and dyed, then corrugated by being squeezed in a heavy wooden press. Leather papers which could be stamped and gilded, were also made. Oiled paper was also in use, made from broussetia paper impregnated with oil from the yegoma plant.

It was no wonder that, with so much variety from which to make a choice, connoisseurship of fine paper developed. Sei Shonagon, a fine court lady born in A.D. 965, went into raptures upon the receipt of a poem from her Empress, written on light green paper. When she received

Nineteenth-century Japanese origami. *The "thousand crane" design is pic-
tured in a pattern book of designs for textiles and other ornamental arts.*
PHOTOGRAPH BY STELLA MAYES REED.

a letter from a lover, written on carnation paper and attached to a bloom of Chinese Pink, she felt life was really worth living—the vehicle of the message was just as important as the message itself. She could never quite bring herself to retire from a world which held such pleasures as the thick white Michinoku paper used for writing letters, "figured white paper, or even plain paper so long as it is pleasing,"[1] or the Imperial paper, of which her Empress, knowing Sei's foibles, sent her twenty rolls.

If paper was sacred to the lover, because it was the vehicle for love letters, or to the Buddhist, because it was the material upon which the sutras were written, it was also sacred to the Shintoist. Strips of folded paper, hanging from a shrine, symbolized the presence of the divinity. They did more; they helped to attract his attention, because it was only by pulling on the paper strip, and thus tinkling a bell, that the god's attention could be called to the prayer of his worshiper. The *gohei*, a sacred scepter decorated with paper foldings, was used in Shinto shrines for purification. Priests wore paper tiaras, which were also occasionally donned by Buddhist clergy for purification ceremonies. The paper folds in Shinto shrines may have been substitutes for offerings of cloth, just as the paper, which always accompanies a gift in Japan, and whose intricate foldings suggest *origami*, may have originally been a silk scarf, like that which always used to accompany a present in Tibet. Not only were the paper decorations associated with religion substitutes for cloth offerings, the paper dolls, and eventually the *origami* which become intertwined with Shintoism are probably substitutes for real human or animal sacrifices.

The Doll's Festival, still observed in Japan, had begun life as a purification ceremony, in which the sins of the community were transferred to scapegoats, personified by paper dolls or *katashiro*. All these religious usages for folded paper built up steam for its emergence as an art form in its own right. At the marriage ceremony, folded paper butterflies symbolized happiness. A. B. Mitford describes how, at a Japanese wedding: "Two married ladies each take one of the wine bottles which have been prepared, and place them in the lower part of the room. The two wine bottles have respectively a male and female butterfly, made of paper, attached to them. The female butterfly is laid on its back, and the wine is poured from the bottle into the kettle. The male butterfly is then taken and laid on the female butterfly, and the wine from the bottle is poured into the same kettle." At a later stage of the ceremonial wedding feast,

<hr />

[1]. Seti Shonagon, *The Pillow Book*, trans. Ivan Morris (London: Penguin Books, 1967), p. 358 and passim.

"butterflies of gold and silver paper are attached to the wine kettles."[2] At some period *origami* paper cranes, called *sembra zuru*—"thousand cranes"—folded in a familiar *origami* design, began to be offered as a silent prayer at the Azumamaru Shrine at Fushimi, Kyoto. Similar *origami* cranes can be seen there today. Not only the Shinto follower, but the Buddhist as well, folded paper charms and prayers, called *miyamairi fuda*, in a particular fashion, and hung them up in temples such as the Yasaka Shrine in Kyoto.

From the sphere of religion, paper folding moved into that of ceremony. The sword smith hung up over his forge a sacred curtain of paper foldings before he donned ceremonial costume and proceeded to carry out the essential part of the task of forging a sword. Paper foldings entered the wrestling ring. Attached to one of the corner pillars was hung a wand, similar to a *gohei*, bearing folded paper of five colors, symbolizing the Five Grains. Like swordsmithery, wrestling partook of a religious rite. It had been instituted as an invocation of the gods to ensure an abundant harvest. To a few champion wrestlers, only two or three in each generation, was given the right to wear a straw rope with paper pendants, an honor conferred by the *Bungo no Kami*, the hereditary arbiter of wrestling in Japan.

More commonplace actions also came to be accompanied by the folded paper of ceremonial usage. *Noshi* and *mizuhiki* were pieces of dried abalone, accompanied by pieces of folded paper in special shapes that were tied with red, white, or gold strings and were gifts at ceremony. The color of the paper was determined by whether the gift was presented on a happy occasion, or a sad one. The shapes of the paper foldings varied a little from time to time, but usually looked much more realistic than pieces of *origami* purposely created to suggest living objects.

Even an ordinary letter was folded in a special way, determined by the rules of etiquette. When, in the seventeenth century, Sakura, a heroic village headman, living on the estates of the Hotta family, decided to petition the Shogun against the raising of the land tax which was ruining his fellow villagers, he knew he had condemned himself and his family to death. Nevertheless, if the Japanese artist who illustrated the story of this village hero is to be believed, he was careful to fold his petition correctly. No doubt, unless it had been folded up properly, the Shogun would have simply refused to receive it. The illustrations to his tragic history show him handing in the neatly folded letter, and then, after the little tyrant of his native fields has secured him once more and crucified him, returning to haunt his lord, still holding the petition.

2. A. B. Mitford *Tales of Old Japan* (London: Macmillan, 1883), pp. 367, 368.

Sakura prepares to hand in his neatly folded petition to the Shogun. Nineteenth-century woodcut. PHOTOGRAPH BY STELLA MAYES REED.

The ghost of Sakura still clutches his carefully folded petition. Nineteenth-century Japanese woodcut. PHOTOGRAPH BY STELLA MAYES REED.

Another sort of life and death petition was a love letter. From Heian times it had become customary to fold such letters in a variety of ways. They could be knotted round the branch of a tree, such as a maple, or a sweet herb, like iris root. In a rather similar way, the horoscopes which the faithful had cast for them in temples were knotted to the bosses of the door of the shrine. They can be seen attached in this way to the door of the shrine of Hachiman at Kyoto. Temple horoscopes are also knotted to the latticework or offering boxes of temples. The color of a letter knotted to the wand of a tree had to correspond to the leaves of the tree. It had to be red for a maple, and so on. Some letters were folded and twisted to produce a fish tail ending, a beautiful formal piece of *origami*.

There was, therefore, no need to "create" *origami*. Like Topsy in *Uncle Tom's Cabin* it "just grew." All that was necessary was to divert the beautiful paper foldings which existed, at least by A.D. 784, from religious and ceremonial uses to amusement. The transition was not a difficult one to effect. A paper stork, hung up in a temple as a supplication, like the storks which can be seen hanging in the Kiyosu kojin temple at Takarazuka, are exactly like those made as toys to amuse children, just as the famous Daruma doll, a bobbing doll which refuses to stay down when pushed over, bears a strong resemblance to statues of the austere hermit, Daruma, in temples.

Nevertheless, the transition took a long time to come about, possibly because life was too serious an affair for much time to be spent amusing children until the comparative peace and prosperity of the eighteenth-century Tokugawa rule. *Origami*, in the shape of formal paper foldings, arrives in the eighth century. Not till the eighteenth century does the first textbook on the subject appear. Most text books on *origami* published after that date give instructions on how to make one, or, at the most, two or three types of folds. One of them, *Hiden Sembazuru Orikata*, published in 1799, deals with the ever-popular folded crane. It gives instructions for making the crane by using just one sheet of paper, without any cutting. Many *origami* artists still believe that this is the correct approach.

The sections of the encyclopedia *Kan no Mado*, a work of uncertain date, but probably eighteenth century, which deal with *origami*, give instructions which sound like a paper sculpture manual. The reader is told to cut the paper to form his models and also to paint them to make them more lifelike. The author of the *origami* section, one Katsuyuki Adachi, evidently felt that models so created would be more attractive to the young—which, in fact, they would. Like Basche, Katsuyuki is very interested in the educational effect of paper craft. He mentions that certain types of *origami* patterns are great favorites with children, patterns which include the "thousand cranes," a boat, and an offering tray. However, education must come before pleasure, and he begins by outlining the paper folds requisite in ceremonies performed according to the Ogasawara school of etiquette. These include the wedding butterflies, called *ocho* and *mecho*, used on festive occasions such as the Boy's Festival, the Boar's Day Observance, and so on.

Katsuyuki himself evidently revels in the more difficult and intricate patterns, and he tends to dismiss the more lifelike ones as child's play.

Interest in *origami* in America and Europe is often felt to have begun in the 1920s, when the American anthropologist, Professor Frederick Starr, drew attention to the pastime in a historic article. As I have already suggested, however, *origami* had been made in America and England long before the twentieth century, only it was called "paper magic," or some similar term. Percy Bysshe Shelley used to amuse himself by folding paper. Lewis Carroll the author of *Alice In Wonderland*, used to take the material for *origami* with him in a special box when he went on train journeys. If he sat next to a child he would take out the box and make some *origami* to amuse his traveling companion. He once entertained the children of the Duke of Albany, a member of the

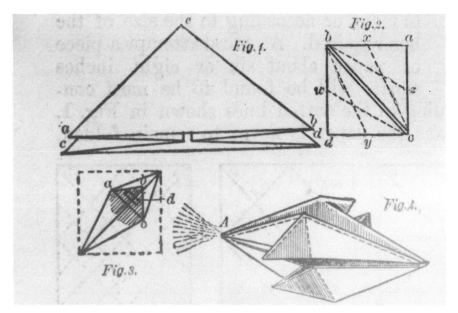

Victorian English origami. *A paper bellows.* PHOTOGRAPH BY STELLA MAYES REED.

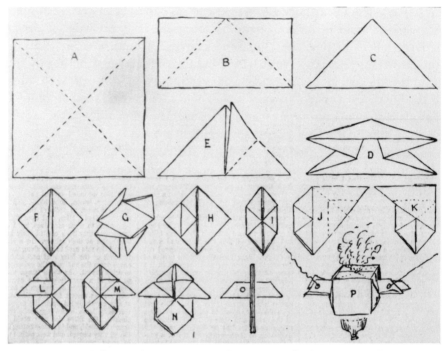

Victorian English origami. *A paper kettle in which one can boil water.*
PHOTOGRAPH BY STELLA MAYES REED.

royal family, by showing them how to make fishing boats and paper pistols.

However clever Carroll might have been at *origami*, he never had to earn a living by it. In Victorian London, street performers in *origami* drew crowds by exhibiting a most ingenious all-purpose *origami* piece called "The Magic Fan," or the "Puzzle Wit." The basic shape of this *origami* creation was a piece of pleated paper that looked just like an ordinary folded fan. A mere twist of the hand, however, converted it into one of many different shapes. "It is said," wrote a Victorian commentator, "that as many as from sixty to seventy varieties have been produced." Common variations of the Magic Fan included mushrooms, Chinese lanterns, wineglasses, wheels, and butter coolers. "Experiment freely on the Magic Fan," wrote the craft writer quoted above. "If spoiled, it costs nothing, but a little patience and a few minutes of time to re-make and a dexterous lad will produce stair-cases, sofas, chairs, flower pots, windows, and window blinds, night caps, boxes, etc."[3]

Victorian *origami* numbered many models, just as ingenious as the

3. Cassells, *Book of Sports and Pastimes,* p. 804.

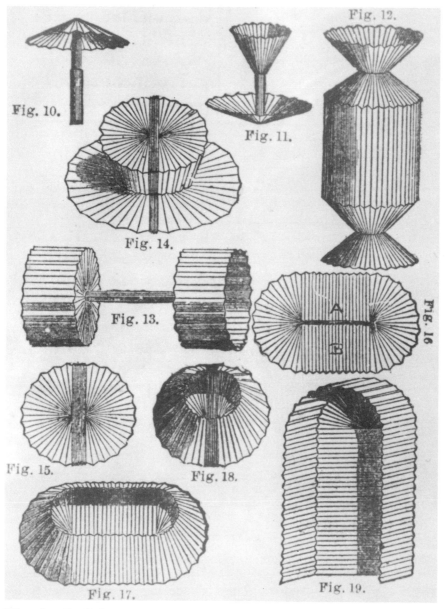

Victorian English origami. *The magic fan.* PHOTOGRAPH BY STELLA MAYES REED.

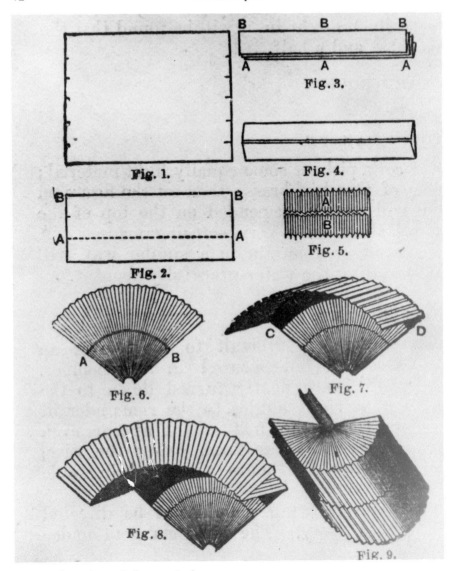

Fig. 1.

Fig. 3.

Fig. 2.

Fig. 4.

Fig. 5.

Fig. 6.

Fig. 7.

Fig. 8.

Fig. 9.

Another view of the magic fan. PHOTOGRAPH BY STELLA MAYES REED.

Magic Fan, if less elaborate. They include paper bellows that really blow, a paper Chinese junk—one of the most complicated and difficult of all the paper toys to make—paper hats, paper boxes, paper purses, paper boats, and even a paper kettle in which you could really boil water over the fire.

Just when European *origami* was in its death throes, when it had dwindled to just one popular art form, the paper dart still thrown by

Modern Japanese origami. COURTESY JAPANESE EMBASSY, LONDON.

school children, it began to revive in America. There must now be many more text books on the subject in English than in Japanese. The best of the moderns, artists like Samuel Randlett, have made their creations known to the public. The secrets of the traditional origamists are also being unearthed, one by one, but it is a sad and striking commentary on how little countries know of the history of their own art that no one in America or England has as yet tried to revive the traditional paper art of the last century.

3

The Eastern Paper Cut

*I*N the Far East, paper cutting took a very different direction from that which it followed in Europe. Much more of an applied than a fine art, it is associated with the shadow theatre, with layouts for all sorts of artisan's designs and with a sturdy peasant creativity very different from the professional artistry which characterizes much paper work in the West. One seemingly trivial reason why paper cutting is very much an art of the people in China and Japan is that the intellectual Chinese had no reason ever to handle a knife—unless he decided to carve himself a brush pot. His tools as a scholar and calligrapher included brushes, ink, an ink slab, water dropper, pen rest, and paper, but no penknife or scissors. The fact that Europeans needed to trim their quill pens with a knife, and the writing box of a Muslim scholar included a special knife for cutting his reed pen, as well as scissors to cut his paper, accounts for the fact that in Europe, paper cutting was a hobby of princes, and that in Turkey, intellectuals produced wonderful calligraphic cutouts. Chinese Emperors might condescend to write a peasant-style ballad, but they would never make a paper cut, because they lacked the essential tools and the skill to use them.

The ordinary Chinese, whether he lived in country or town, was an extremely clever craftsman. With his knife he could even carve himself a pair of bamboo scissors which would actually cut paper—a feat no one else has ever been able to achieve.

The popularity which paper enjoyed almost as soon as it was invented in China as a decorative element in funerals ensured that it would find

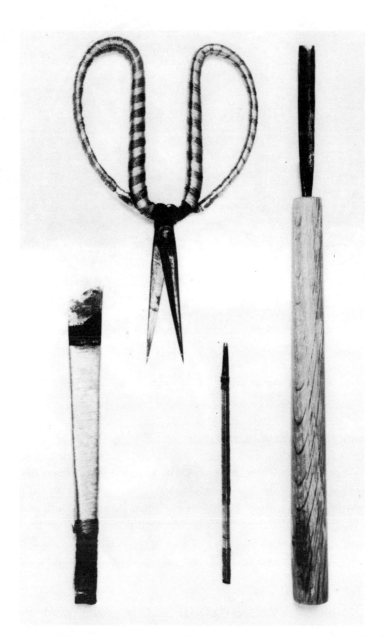

Tools of the Chinese paper cutter. Top: scissors. Right: punch. Left: knife. Middle: small punch. COURTESY HORNIMAN MUSEUM, LONDON.

Chinese paper cut, Shangtung. Contemporary. COURTESY HORNIMAN MU-
SEUM, LONDON.

a use on more everyday occasions as well. By the Tang Dynasty (618-
713) emperors and courtiers decked themselves in gold and silver paper
"Spring Flags," for the Spring Festival, or Chinese New Year, and paper
decorations were part of a woman's accessories, just as they were, until
very recently, for Turkish brides. The house, and garden, were also
adorned with paper ornaments. Courtiers and poets (such as the famous
Su Tung-Po) continued to wear cutout decorations during the Sung
Dynasty (960-1279) but already the pleasures of the rich had become
those of the poor as well.

From the moment it was invented, paper must have seemed the in-
dispensable substitute for the material used for glazing windows, which
was probably sheets of processed intestine or parchment. Paper was
cheap, and easily stretched and pasted, when wet, over a wooden frame.
Because of their low cost, the paper windows were renewed every year
on the occasion of the Spring Festival or Chinese New Year. Their
new whiteness, like the whiteness of a freshly whitewashed Polish home
on the occasion of that great Polish festival, Easter, seemed to cry out

Chinese paper cut, Hopei. Contemporary. COURTESY HORNIMAN MUSEUM, LONDON.

for colored decoration. A legendary heroine of the tenth century, Lady Yi, had become famous for having traced, with a brush and ink, the shadows of the bamboo leaves on her paper window. Humbler Chinese housewives could have told her that an applied paper decoration would be much more practical than a printed one, because if you wet a tightly stretched paper window you risk breaking it. (The traditional way to make a peephole in a paper window in China or Japan is to apply to it a wet forefinger.) So with every Spring Festival new paper decorations replaced the old ones on the windows.

Something has already been said about the religious associations of paper in the Far East. In China, "door gods" cut out in paper early began to decorate houses—as they still do in Japan. *Tou-siang-hua*, or sacrificial incense flowers, were also cut from paper as early as the eighth century, to be burned as offerings in shrines. Other paper cutouts, such as those made in Juang-tung, were burned as a funeral sacrifice, like spirit money.

Chinese women or male artisans turned out paper cutouts as designs.

Chinese paper cut, Chekiang. Contemporary. COURTESY HORNIMAN MUSEUM, LONDON.

Chinese paper cut, Kiangsu. Contemporary. COURTESY HORNIMAN MUSEUM, LONDON.

Chinese paper cut, Chekiang. Contemporary. COURTESY HORNIMAN MUSEUM, LONDON.

One of the most popular uses for "flower patterns" was as designs for embroidery. A girl making her hope chest would create her own embroidery patterns if she were able; if not she would buy them from a professional cutter. These men were known in China by the poetical name of "pilgrims of lakes and rivers," a high-sounding title which did not compensate them for the hardships of their very precarious livelihood. They could be found at fairs, in vegetable markets, or in temple courtyards. Often their whole families had helped them to prepare the paper cuts with which they wandered about from place to place. They mass-produced these cuts by laying a pile of thin paper sheets on a plank and nailing them down. They then cut round the design very carefully with a knife, selecting a different knife for the cut required. In the "way of the knife," lay the whole whole secret of the cutter's art. There was no preliminary sketching, the cutter carried the pattern in his head, just as a Chinese painter carried the outline of his drawing. A few simple punches, such as those which Constantin suggested would be of use to the eighteenth-century French amateur cutter, completed the paper artist's equipment. Their customers preferred colored cutouts to white ones—naturally enough, seeing that what was the color of mourning.

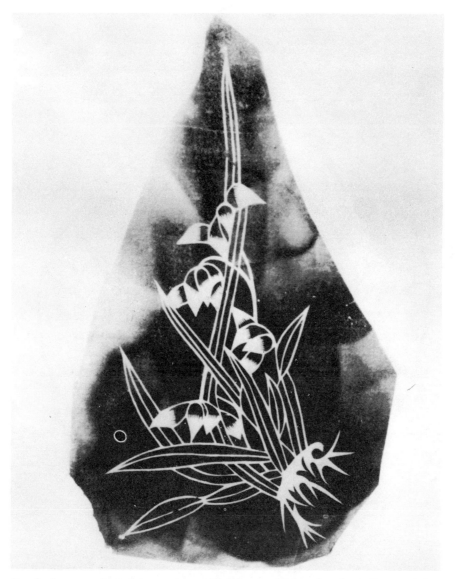

Smoked copy of paper cut from Chekiang. A cut that is to be copied is pasted lightly onto a piece of paper and held over a candle flame or the flame of an oil lamp. The smoke makes a perfect copy. COURTESY HORNIMAN MUSEUM, LONDON.

Chinese paper cut, Shangtung. Contemporary. COURTESY HORNIMAN MU-
SEUM, LONDON.

Chinese paper cut, Kwangtung. Contemporary. COURTESY HORNIMAN MU-
SEUM, LONDON.

The professional cutters were able to dye numbers of cuts at a time
by laying a number of sheets on top of one another and flooding the top
of the stack with a brushful of liquid dye, which would gradually perco-
late through the sheets. Embroidery patterns were always sold in pairs,
because twin patterns would secure the symmetrical effect so desired in
Chinese embroidery, in which one design, such as the character for
"good luck," for example, appears on the front of a jacket, with an
identical character design on the back. Once it was used for embroidery,
the design could not be used again, because it was pasted onto the material and sewn round and round till it was completely enclosed in the
embroided stitches. However, a girl who wanted to keep a copy of an
embroidery pattern could do so very easily by pasting it lightly to a
sheet of white paper, and holding it for a few moments over the flame
of a lamp. Once the original pattern was peeled off the paper the design
would appear, in reverse, as a white-on-black print.

Closely allied to the embroidery pattern in use and design was the stencil for dyeing cloth in blue patterns by the batik process. The home-spun cotton used for women's and children's garments was spread out and on it was laid a stencil cut from oiled paper. A paste of water and lime was then brushed through the holes of the stencil and left to dry. Next the bolt of cotton was dyed with indigo, and finally the white paste was scraped off. This process left white designs, on the blue, wherever the resist designs had been brushed on. Stencils for dyeing incorporated the same kinds of symbolic designs which were to be found in embroidery patterns, designs which included the "dog of Fo" (Buddha), which warded off evil influences, and locks which chained the spirit of a child to earth. Because the design had to cover the whole area of the cotton print, it was repeated again and again. The lines of the stencil

Chinese paper cut, Kiangsu. Contemporary. COURTESY HORNIMAN MUSEUM, LONDON.

Chinese paper cut, Hopei. Contemporary. COURTESY HORNIMAN MUSEUM, LONDON.

Chinese paper cut, Hopei. Contemporary. COURTESY HORNIMAN MUSEUM, LONDON.

were robust, without any of the spidery thinness characteristic of many embroidery patterns, for the brush and the solvent lime would have easily abraded too delicate a line.

Embroidery and stencil designs are easily the most important of all paper cuts, because their designs have survived from the earliest times that paper was in use. The same can be said of the resist paper designs pasted onto porcelain before it was covered with a colored glaze and fired. The paper pattern would be destroyed completely, but the outline of its design was fired onto the porcelain forever, white in relief against the colored background.

By contrast with industrial designs, paper cuts *per se* were as ephemeral as spirit money. The only ones we know anything about are those made during the recent years of the twentieth century.

The Spring Festival happy greetings, pasted on doors for the New Year, were only intended to last for a year, yet they might take the most elaborate forms, incorporating collage with small printed engravings stuck to the paper. Colors and gold and silver paper enhanced their festive appearance. Some of the most artistic, however, are spidery, delicate cuts made from the red paper of congratulation. They often

Chinese paper cut, Hopei. Contemporary. COURTESY HORNIMAN MUSEUM, LONDON.

Chinese paper cut, Kiangsu. Contemporary. COURTESY HORNIMAN MUSEUM, LONDON.

Chinese paper cut, North West Provinces. Contemporary. COURTESY HORNI-MAN MUSEUM, LONDON.

Chinese paper cut, North West Provinces. Contemporary. COURTESY HORNI-MAN MUSEUM, LONDON.

Chinese paper cut, Kwangtung. Contemporary. COURTESY HORNIMAN MU-SEUM, LONDON.

Chinese paper cut, Kwangtung. Contemporary. COURTESY HORNIMAN MU-SEUM, LONDON.

Chinese paper cut, Nanking. Contemporary. COURTESY HORNIMAN MUSEUM, LONDON.

Chinese paper cut, Nanking. Contemporary. COURTESY HORNIMAN MUSEUM, LONDON.

incorporate characters such as *shung hsi*, "double joy," and symbols that, before the Communist regime, often emphasized prosperity: coins, rolls of money, and horses and carts laden with cash.

The "window flowers," decorative cutouts pasted onto the paper windows, have been referred to previously. Like so many other forms of Chinese art, they were extremely practical. They masked the shadows thrown directly onto the windows, for the moment darkness fell, every Chinese house became a shadow theater. There were no curtains, and all privacy was lost unless the silhouettes of the occupants were disrupted by the paper decorations.

Ornamental cutouts of congratulation, called "happiness flowers," or *si-hua*, were attached to presents, like the *noshi* used in Japan.

Besides incorporating many diverse subjects, such as flowers, birds, animals, folklore, scenes from everyday life, Chinese characters, the theater, and literature, paper cut designs were heavily charged with symbolism. A picture of a *Kylin*, a legendary unicorn, for example, conveyed the wish that the wearer of the garment would bear many children. As in Poland, there were many regional variations. Paper cuts made in

Chinese paper cut, Nanking. Contemporary. COURTESY HORNIMAN MUSEUM, LONDON.

Chinese paper cut, North West Provinces. Contemporary. COURTESY HORNIMAN MUSEUM, LONDON.

Chinese paper cut, Chekiang. Contemporary. COURTESY HORNIMAN MUSEUM, LONDON.

the North were usually enclosed in a surrounding frame—which was not necessary to the embroidery when it was carried out. Southern paper cuts were free standing. They could take the form of good luck wishes, which the vendor would cut out for you while you waited, horses tethered in bamboo groves, and water buffaloes pulling ploughs. It has been suggested that paper cuts were simpler and more robust in the North, more delicate and gorgeous in the South. Wherever they were made, Chinese paper cuts seem to bear the light delicate touch of a woman's hand. If they were not all made by women, a great many of them were made for women, and perhaps they are woman's most notable contribution to art.

The Chinese shadow theater popularized the idea of paper cuts throughout China. As early as the Sung Dynasty, ordinary people in the capital of Piangliang, crowded after dark to see and hear the plays given by the shadow puppeteers, plays which incorporated folklore and popular ballads, but which perforce had to have a cast of shadow puppets of men, women and animals. Stylistically speaking there is a good deal of resemblance between the puppets and paper cuts in China. Both have patterned bodies, even though, in the case of the puppets, these patterns are painted onto the transparent donkey hide, or oiled paper, with transparent colors, and in the cutouts, the designs are cut with a knife. Both puppets and cutouts can accommodate the same kind of themes: historical personages, mythical animals, scenes from real life, and so on.

Is it being too fanciful to see, in the shadow puppets created in Egypt, which no doubt receive their original inspiration from China, via Persia, a Chinese-type lattice-work decoration which vaguely recalls that used in the *Liber Passionis*?

Although Japan did not adopt the shadow theater, it accepted the paper cut, and used it as a vehicle for its own very national art. Paper cuts, or *sagegami*, as they are called in Japan, are still used to decorate Buddhist altars and house doorways at the Chinese New Year or Spring Festival. These paper cuts convey the same kind of messages as did the old Chinese paper cuts. Congratulatory wishes and good luck characters are employed, together with carp (the symbol of persistence overcoming difficulties) Not all the themes are purely Chinese, however; some represent concepts which no Chinese would ever have heard of, such as the Lucky Treasure Ship, and the Seven Gods Of Luck, particularly Daikoku and Ebisu, the gods of wealth and prosperity. No one could ever mistake a Japanese paper cut, such as those made in Sado, in Niigata, for its Chinese equivalent. Though I have used rather a stumpy, fat, cut as an illustration, it must not be forgotten that here the shape of the character has determined the shape of the cut. In the majority of Japanese cuts

Nineteenth-century Japanese stencil of a goldfish. PHOTOGRAPH BY STELLA MAYES REED.

Nineteenth-century Japanese stencil of umbrellas and crests with the names of their owners. PHOTOGRAPH BY STELLA MAYES REED.

Nineteenth-century Japanese stencil of chrysanthemums. PHOTOGRAPH BY
STELLA MAYES REED.

Nineteenth-century Japanese stencil. Splashed design. PHOTOGRAPH BY STELLA
MAYES REED.

Nineteenth-century Japanese stencil of crayfish. PHOTOGRAPH BY STELLA MAYES REED.

however, great restraint has been used and just a few tiny cuts have been sufficient to etch in the whole picture.

A glance at a Japanese paper cut will reveal its relationship to the stencil. No more elaborate and sophisticated stencils have ever been devised than those created by the Japanese stencil cutters. According to tradition, the stencil cut from a sheet of thick paper was introduced into Japan by a dyer named Someya Yuzen, toward the end of the seventeenth century. Stencils were, however, almost certainly in use in some crafts before this date, in lacquer work, for example. It is quite possible, however, that Someya did introduce the more elaborate kind of stencil designed for dyeing polychrome fabrics.

Stencils were made up, thriftily, from old documents pasted together. Already by 1825 the Japanese stenciler was producing work which looked like a pin-prick picture, and fabrics printed from such stencils may have helped to popularize pin-prick in Europe.

The great American scholar, Andrew Tuer, the first person to investigate Japanese stencils, has given a classic exposition of their construction: "The artist-workman takes some half-dozen sheets of tough paper made of mulberry fiber (*Broussonetia papyrifera*) prepared with the juice of persimmon and waterproofed with a hard drying oil. On the top he places the artist's design, drawn with ink. The sheets firmly secured, he begins cutting with a long thin knife which he pushes before him in the same way as a copperplate engraver at home uses the burin. Slowly and accurately the keen blade cuts through the little pile of paper, following the curves of the design. Where there are punctured holes or dots the knife is superceded by a fine punch, for if pins were used a burr would be formed and the design would not print clean and sharp.

"Through necessary cutting away, some of the finer or more delicately designed stencils are so fragile that there is not enough paper left to hold them together. These are strengthened by the addition of silk threads stretched at regular intervals from top to bottom and from side to side. The threads are so fine that the stencil brush ignores them and they leave no mark; and the mesh or net they form is so strong, and withal so delicate, that a spider might have woven it.

"When the cutting out is finished, two of the sheets are damped so that they may expand and, what is of equal importance, contract equally in drying. One is laid down flat and covered with adhesive material. The threads are then one by one put in position, the ends sticking onto the margins. Each plate has at top or bottom two small punctures which

Nineteenth-century Japanese stencil. Chrysanthemums and willow design.
PHOTOGRAPH BY STELLA MAYES REED.

Nineteenth-century Japanese stencil of storks. PHOTOGRAPH BY STELLA MAYES REED.

Japanese paper cut used for New Year celebrations. It incorporates the character Takava (*treasure*).

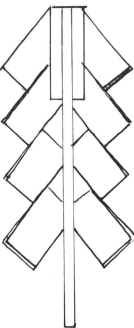

Gohei. *The emblem in a Shinto shrine which represents the ancient cloth offerings.*

form no part of the design; these are register marks. The second stencil is accurately laid over the first by means of upright pins placed in the register holes, the two paper plates are brought exactly together and the threads securely imprisoned. The joining of the two plates enclosing the thread is so absolutely perfect that a strong glass fails to disclose any sign of overlapping or unevenness."

Once the paper cutter had finished one pile of stencils, he put a stenciled impression on top of the next pile as a guide, and went on cutting the same design until he had as many stencils as he required.

Though the dyer used a large soft brush which yielded to the slightest pressure, his frail stencils cannot have lasted long, and probably the only ones to survive are those hailed by Tuer, and his fellow American connoisseur, S. Bing, as great works of art in paper. Collectors, such as Mrs. Ernest Hart, framed stencils by placing them upon a piece of white or tinted paper to throw up the design, and Bing's reproduction of many of these "Industrial Models," in the illustrations to his journal, *Artistic Japan* incorporated the traditional skill of the Japanese paper cutter into the artistic heritage of the West.

Those countries in touch with China, such as Turkey, began to develop their own paper art at an early date due to the inspiration of Chinese work. By the sixteenth century there was a craft guild in Constantinople, "who made all sorts of carved work in paper." In 1582, as the guildsmen of the city marched past the Sultan, the paper cutters carried as their display, "a very beautiful garden, and a castle decorated with flowers made of multicoloured papers, artistically cut."[1]

It is difficult to guess, just from this description, whether paper sculpture, collage, or even découpage is referred to here. The *Book of the divan* of *Mehmed Selim*, which is now in the library of Nedjib Pacha at Tiré, near Smyrna, is ornamented with collages of different colored paper. The decorative motifs used are vases filled with flowers, very similar in style to the painted panels ornamenting the upper parts of the walls of the *yali* of the Koprulu family at Anadolou Hisar on the Bosporus. They resemble somewhat Mrs. Delany's flower mosaic.

[1] Quoted in Christian Rubi, *Cut Paper Silhouettes and Stencils* (London: Kaye and Ward).

4

Découpage

R EGULAR découpage was carried out in Turkey under the name
of *Kat'i*. The subjects generally employed by the paper cutters (who
were called *Katta*) were vases of flowers, stylized landscapes, verses
of the Koran, or maxims, written in the best calligraphic style. A typical
chef d'oeuvre of the *katta* might take the form of a pear-shaped composition containing a phrase such as *aman mürürvet*, arranged in flow-
ing calligraphy. The cutouts, which were made from colored paper, were
stuck onto a cardboard background. They were then framed like pictures, or preserved in chests, wrapped in silk or brocade.

Turkish découpage bears a very close relationship to calligraphy because the tools of the paper cutter were also those of the calligrapher.
The paper on which a scribe wrote was sold to him by the sheet; he had
to cut it to shape himself. Different kinds of communication demanded
a different size of paper—as late as the middle of the nineteenth century,
five principal sizes of paper were designated by the Ottoman government
for particular kinds of state papers—so the scribe would get plenty of
practice in paper cutting. The little box in which the scribe carried his
equipment would contain a pair of sharp scissors with long points to cut
the paper, for a torn edge was considered unbecoming. It would also
contain a penknife with a long handle and a short blade with an oblique
point, rather like a *canivet* (the word means "little knife"). An even
smaller penknife might be tucked into the sheath of the large one. When
he could afford it, a calligrapher would buy knives which had been

forged out of the best tempered steel by some sword smith of renown. The scribe also used a tiny cutting block of ivory or bone, on which to trim his pens. This could serve as a base to cut paper on in the way described by Constantin.

It is not surprising, then, that in Turkey, as in Europe, the mechanical day to day task of cutting paper to the required sizes and trimming pens into shape brought about the artistic development of paper cutting as a fine art. The fact that Turkish professional paper cutters are already organized in a guild during the sixteenth century at a time when the art is still in its infancy in Europe suggests that European découpage may owe at least some of its inspiration to that carried on in the Ottoman Empire, while Turkey may have derived its paper art through Persia from China, the original home of paper and paper cutting.

In view of the large part that England is going to play in paper craft, it is not altogether surprising to find that the first important work of découpage, or paper cutting, known to have survived, has strong English associations. It is the *Book of the Passion*, now in the library of the Princesse de Ligne, in Belgium, a book made for the English king, Henry VII. This magnificent piece of découpage has been cut, not in paper, but in vellum. The method of decoration, however, is identical with that subsequently applied to paper. All the characters in the book are cut out with a knife. The same technique can be seen applied to such a late paper cut as an epitaph on Alexander II of Russia, written in English and preserved in the British Museum.

In spite of its very early date—1500 is the year attributed to it in a later rebinding—and the fact that it came from what was then a very out of the way and artistically backward country, which was only just beginning to feel the stirrings of the Renaissance, the *Book of Passion*, is a masterpiece which has never been equaled, much less surpassed, in the whole history of découpage. Its proud owners, the Princes de Linge, knew its value well, and set the highest store by it. In 1611 the Prince of the day, Lamoral, entailed it on his eldest male descendant, along with the jewels he had received from Philip III of Spain, and the diamonds which had passed into the family through Louise de Foix. A later Prince, Albert Henri, described it in his catalogue of the family library as: *"The Book of the Passion of Our Lord Jesus Christ* with pictures and characters composed of nothing."[1] He also noted in the catalogue that his predecessor, Lamoral, had refused an offer of 11,000 gold crowns made for the book by the Emperor Rudolph.

The *Book of the Passion*, is quite a small book, about seven and a

---

[1] G. Magnien, *Canivets, Découpures and Silhouetttes* (Lyons, 1947), p. 4.

half by five and a half inches opened out. It is made from the finest and
whitest vellum, each vellum leaf alternating with one of blue paper.
Passages of text in Latin, giving the account of the Passion according
to St. John's Gospel, are interspersed with whole page ornaments of cutwork, pictures, and a heraldic dedicatory page. This displays the arms
of Henry VII of England, surmounted by his crown and surrounded by
the ribbon of the Garter, bearing the royal motto: *Hony soyt qui mal y
pense*. Minute Tudor roses punctuate the words of the motto. Tudor
roses, and that other royal badge, the Portcullis, figure on the arched
frame, supported on two pillars, which bears the royal arms.

Facing the dedicatory page is the frontispiece, and arch-shaped ornamentation of incredibly fine cutwork which recalls the latticed windows
of Islamic mosque decoration.

Cutwork pictures follow, representing the kiss given by Judas, the
flagellation, the crowning with thorns, Jesus on the Cross, his death, and
his entombment. As it stands, the *Liber Passionis*, to give it its Latin
title, seems to be incomplete, but there can be no doubt that it was a
custom-built book, specifically intended to be presented to Henry VII
of England. Henry was a miser given to occasional acts of magnificence,
such as the tomb which he commissioned from the Italian, Torrigiano,
which can still be seen in Westminster Abbey. Was the *Liber Passionis*
another of his occasional lapses into extravagance? Was it a piece of
applied art made by a great artistic calligrapher, the masterpiece of some
craftsman of genius, the dedicated labor of a monk in a cloister, or the
pastime of some noble prisoner, who sought perhaps to obtain Henry's
favor, and his release from captivity, by a gift worthy of a prince? All
that one can be certain of is that the *Liber Passionis* is such a beautiful
book that anyone who saw it would long to own some similar work. The
tradition of vellum, cutting established by such books may have encouraged the subjects of Henry's granddaughter, Elizabeth I, to take up
artistic vellum cutting.

Work of this sort would be an inspiration not merely to vellum artists,
but to those who cut paper as well. It is possible to think of examples of
paper cutting, similar in style, if not in date, to the *Liber Passionis*. They
include a bookmark figuring a Crucifixion, ornamented with dice,
scourges, ladders, and a crowing cock, and bearing the signature:
"Verfertick L. Broc," which was once owned by the late Desmond Coke.

Vellum and paper cutting continued to exist side by side. In France,
another Henry, Henri III, ordered a service book rather on the lines of
Henry VII's *Book of the Passion*. If the *Liber Passionis* had found its
way to the continent by that time, possibly as part of the dowry of

Henry's daughter, Mary, who married the king of France, Henri may even have looked at it, and been attracted by the decorations which employed the crowned "H," a decoration that he himself might have adopted. At any rate, after Henri had established the *Ordre du Saint Esprit*, a royal order of honor, in December, 1578, he commissioned a *Book of Hours*. The text, which is in Latin and French, is cut out with a knife, as in the *Liber Passionis*, and is bound in a similar way. An olive colored backing paper is placed behind each page, while a double gold band frames each page and separates one line of text from another. It may seem incredible that anyone could undertake such a laborious task as the cutting out of each letter in a book with a knife. This, however, was how the work was carried out. Slight irregularities in the letters of the *Liber Passionis*—the thicknesses of the letter "I" for example— prove that no punch was used. Nor, apparently, was any preliminary drawing or writing done on the parchment before the letters were cut out with a knife.

Exquisite *découpe* decoration in vellum was made in the seventeenth century for private books of devotion, such as the *megillah*, or *Book of Esther*, used by some Jewish communities in Italy. Strict religious rules governed the decoration and calligraphy which could be employed on the Rolls of the Law used in the Synagogue. No *sopherim* or scribes would have dared to ornament them according to their artistic fancies, any more than a Muslim calligrapher writing the Koran would have

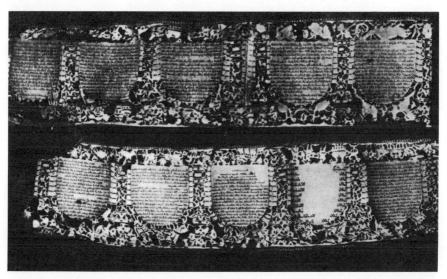

Jewish parchment cutwork Book of Esther, made in Italy in the seventeenth century. POTOGRAPH BY STELLA MAYES REED.

chosen to use elaborate Persian flourishes. The scribes found a freer vent for their artistic impulses by preparing *Books of Esther*, such as a roll which vies with the *Liber Passionis* for first place in the whole history of découpage. This roll, now in the Roth Collection in Jerusalem, is apparently identical with one formerly owned by Mr. A. Hewett, the Mayor of Richmond, England, which was described by Mrs. E. Nevill Jackson in her book *Silhouette*. The roll, which is four yards long and just over six inches wide, is mounted on red silk and has an edging made of passement, added in the eighteenth century. Arch-shaped medallions (which remind us of the arch-shaped decorations of the *Liber Passionis*) are interspersed with groups of figures in seventeenth-century dress, who act out Old Testament scenes, such as the hanging of Haman's sons, with floral arabesques, dogs, lions, crocodiles, winged dragons, and many kinds of birds. All these ornaments have a symbolic significance. They appear not just on *megiloth*, or Esther scrolls, (another fine example of which is preserved in the Jewish Museum, London, England) but also on highly ornamented marriage contracts called *ketubbot*, which date from the seventeenth to the nineteenth centuries. These attractive "marriage lines" were often illuminated, as well as having cutwork borders. They are known from countries as far afield as Holland, Alsace, Hungary, Poland, and North Africa.

Christian and Jewish découpage are probably related to one another, and they may stem from a common source of inspiration, perhaps the shadow theater puppets in camel hide vellum prepared by puppeteers in Muslim Egypt between the eleventh and the twelfth centuries. Many of these figures were discovered by Dr. Paul Kahle in the Nile Valley. Vellum cutting and paper cutting are also obviously related as well; however vellum is an expensive material and it is not surprising that most European *découpage* was carried out in paper.

Henri III of France, whom we have already noted commissioning a vellum *Book of Hours* in cutwork, was also a great patron of cut paper. He would sit in the Louvre for hours at a time, surrounded by his gentlemen in waiting, reading his prayer book, and then suddenly seize a knife and begin cutting out pictures of saints. The markedly feminine side of Henri's nature may have helped to interest him in découpage. He was fond of wearing female accessories, such as earrings. He may have also carried one of the parchment fans fashionable at the time. These were rectangular in shape, and ornamented with gold or silver braiding and embroidery. The face of the fan was covered with a sheet of parchment, cut out in ornaments resembling Venice lace. Roses and clover leaf, set in a lacework border, predominated in their decoration, and the découpage was thrown into relief by a backing of brilliantly colored silk, just like the colored pages which acted as a foil for the open cutwork of the vellum prayer books.

Apparently Henri and his *mignons*, or homosexual paramours, also wore paper lace. This at least may be inferred from a note which the Parisian diarist, Pierre de l'Estoile, makes in his journal for 4th February, 1579. Several young students, he tells us, have been walking about the Fair of St. Germains, wearing long paper ruffs, "in mockery of His Majesty and his *mignons*,"[2] and the king has had them arrested. Lace could easily be imitated in paper. The beautiful sixteenth and seventeenth-century French and Flemish lace patterns, such as *point d'Alençon, Malines, Mirecourt,* and *point d'Angleterre* served as inspiration for much of the French découpage which has survived. Experts have even declared that the influence of Breton lace, with its murex shell notifs, can be detected in some paper cutwork, so it may be possible, eventually, to assign many pieces of French découpage to regional schools. Other sources that, it has been claimed, inspired or influenced paper cuts in France, were the floral designs shown on German gilt or painted paper, or the paper patterns for Italian ironwork. Some paper cuts also evolved from children's play. At one time during the era of paper work it became customary to amuse children by giving them old prints of no value and letting them cut out the *white* parts of the design. Paper cuts which look like prints with all the *black* lines cut out were to be made during the eighteenth century by the English paper artist, Nathaniel Bermingham.

The paper cut was called a *canivet* in France, after the tool with which it was made. A *canivet* was a specialized kind of penknife, and it literally was a penknife because it was used for trimming pens made from bird's quill feathers. The *canivet* must have been very similar to those knives which were used for the same purpose in Turkey, and other Muslim countries, and which were called, in Turkish, *kalemtras*. They had steel or silver blades; the silver ones must have been more ornamental than useful. They were set in a horn, wood, ivory, silver, or enameled handle, and the point of the blade was double-edged, like a medical lancet. The blades were very small. Till quite recently, *canivets* were made in Thiers, in France, and sold at the fair there. The Thiers *canivets* had blades measuring only an inch and a half by a quarter of an inch. Other *canivets*, from Bayonne, used for trimming goose quills to make into pens, had been on sale at the Lyons fair as early as 1573.

The paper cuts made with these little knives (no one had yet started

2. Ibid.

to make paper cuts with scissors, which were fairly clumsy tools) were used for various purposes. Some were slipped into the pages of missals to mark the place. This particular use has given paper cuts the name they still retain in the Swiss Vaudois, *marques*. Henri III was fond of using bookmarks and had his mistress portrayed, under the guise of Our Lady, on a bookmark, so that he could look at her face when he was supposed to be at his prayers.

Other *canivets* of small size were used, as early as the seventeenth century at least, to ornament reliquaries. A whole school of convent art grew up around paper. The handicraft of the nuns was to include rolled paper as well as open work, as will be seen in another chapter. Convent work was sufficiently impressive to earn a mention from the *Encyclopédie*. "Paper which is gilded by means of a little leaf of fine gold serves to ornament reliquiaries,"[3] it remarks, "also small devotional pictures and other little works. Nuns carry out the same work in silvered paper. These gold and silver papers . . . are manufactured in Paris. German gilt paper is not imitated in France, for the reason that as copper leaf comes from Germany it would be too dear."

A French author called Furetière tells us that in convents: "The nuns cut parchment in order to make cut paper work representing different figures or designs which are then stuck on wood, velvet, and other materials. The religious ladies and their pupils employ their spare time in making these cut paper pieces."[4]

Though some of the convent work may appear a little naive when set beside the work of a professional artist like Joanna Koerten Blok, the best of it shows real devotional inspiration and tireless application of detail. The late Gabriel Magnien, a great French antiquary who collected and conserved most of the *canivets* which we now possess, can give us little help in explaining just how these beautiful paper pictures were cut. He suggests that the original design might have been marked onto the surface of the paper with the point of a knife before the openwork was cut out. By folding the paper, symmetrical halves of the composition might have been cut through at one time. There appears to be no trace of this having been done.

One of the most interesting features of the *canivet* is its originality. There is so little resemblance between one paper cut and another that if a mother was forced to abandon her child, and leave it outside an orphanage or a convent, she would tear a *canivet* in two, keep one half,

---

3. Ibid., p. 16.
4. Ibid.

and leave the other tucked into the abandoned child's baby clothes. Later, if her circumstances improved, she could prove her claim to the child by producing her half of the paper cut.

Those *canivets* which were not used for reliquaries were often used to frame a picture of a saint. They were mounted on rich brocade or velvet and placed in beautiful maple-wood frames. Other, smaller, canivets were preserved in coffers.

So popular had découpage become by the seventeenth century that the first professional artists known to us by name begin to appear. Two of the most famous are women, the first of whom is Anne Marie de Schurman, born in Cologne in 1607.

"From her infancy," remarks Niceron, "she showed herself to be extraordinarily skillful with her hands, for at the age of six, she made, with her scissors, all sorts of figures on paper, without using any kind of model."[5] Anne Marie had many other talents as well. She composed crayon flower pictures at the age of eight, embroidered beautifully, drew protraits on glass with the point of a diamond, modeled in wax, made artificial pearls so like the real gems that she had to pierce them with a pin to convince her friends that they were not genuine, and wrote such a fine hand that her friends preserved her letters in their albums as master calligraphy. On the 18th of March, 1648, she wrote to Madame de Saumaise of Utrecht. "I here present you with a trial piece by my Muse, and my scissors, in gratitude for the benefits I have received from you."[6]

Anne Marie achieved European fame before her death in 1678, but it is difficult to tell how much of it was due to her découpage and how much to the Latin treaties which she wrote. However, her renown as an artist probably contributed to the careful preservation of many of her cut work pictures. Until the twentieth century, a number of them could be seen in the University of Utrecht. The publication of Anne Marie's protrait, by the Elzevirs, and the many references to her in contemporary letters, may have also helped to popularized the art of paper cutting.

Unlike Anne Marie, who was an amateur, her contemporary, Joanna Koerten (1650-1715) was a professional artist, and a very highly paid one at that. Joanna Koerten Blok, as she is usually called, because she was the wife of Adrien Blok, the artist, was the most highly esteemed and highly rewarded of all known paper cutters. The Empress of Leopold I, Holy Roman Emperor, paid 4,000 florins for a trophy of her

---

5. Ibid., p. 7.
6. Ibid.

husband's coat of arms which Joanna cut. To look at any of her work, such as the Virgin and Child cut by her in 1703, preserved in the Victoria and Albert Museum, London, is to be overwhelmed by the feeling of space, and monumental quality which she succeeds in conveying in a composition small enough to be framed in a locket. The Virgin, Child and St. John are placed in a landscape of incredible minuteness and delicacy. Birds the size of pin heads fly among the trees, all of them quite distinct species, yet so small that the details in the cutting, and the legend written on a band running through the picture, (now reversed in the present mounting) can only be appreciated through a magnifying glass.

Joanna, born in Amsterdam in 1650, had early evinced a taste for the fine arts. She became a capable musician, made beautiful embroidery, modeled fruit and figures, and engraved with a diamond point on crystal and glass with incredible delicacy. She invented new techniques for oil and water color painting, and her friends felt she could have become a great painter had she not given up her other arts to concentrate on paper work.

"All that the engraver accomplishes with the burin," wrote her biographer," she was able to execute with the scissors. Her cuttings were indeed astonishing. Country scenes, marine views, animals, flowers, with portraits of perfect resemblance, she executed in a marvellous manner."

Kings and Queens vied with one another to possess her work. "She had in her working room a volume, in which were registered the names of her illustrious visitors, the princes and princesses and other great personages writing their own."[7] Her husband made portraits of her famous callers, which he attached to the register, opposite their names. He also published a series of vignettes based on her cuttings. Queen Mary, wife of William III, bought specimens of her work and had her portrait made by Joanna. Peter the Great of Russia made a point of calling on her to pay his respects, and her portraits "excited the curiosity of all the courts of Europe." The Elector Palatine, who offered a thousand florins for three of her small cuttings, had his offer spurned because it was not generous enough. When one considers that the Virgin and Child, with St. John, is so small and so fragile and only measures two and three quarter inches in height, it is easy to see how so many of Joanna's masterpieces have been lost.

The subjects of Joanna's cuttings correspond quite closely to the kind of paper cuts which were on sale at the shop of Van Vliet of Rotterdam in 1687, where there could be bought "curious works of

7. Ibid.

ships, palaces, and landscapes, made and shaped solely with the point of a knife."[8]

By this date several specialized types of paper cuttings had begun to emerge. One was the paper ship. A good example was cut by Queen Anne of England and presented to one of her court, in whose family it was long treasured. Cut-out paper ships of this sort often bore a motto, as does one in Lyons Museum, such as "I repose after the dangers I have passed, *Post pericula quiesco*." The landscape was another favorite theme. It had a long life ahead of it and it was to be very popular with folk artists. Heraldic cutouts were also particularly favored—we have seen that some of Joanna Koerten's work took this form. There is a good example of a heraldic cutting in the Tafel Collection at Stuttgart. It bears the date 1631, and is signed by Johannes David Schaffer. The cutting depicts a triumphal car with angels, heraldic arms, animals, and symbols. A very fine heraldic emblem, formerly in the late Captain Desmond Coke's collection, also shows child angels who support a shield. A French origin is suggested by the legend running on a scroll at the bottom of the picture: *La vertue et la sagesse conduisent au bonheur*—"Virtue and wisdom lead to happiness." The beautifully cut flowers which surround the angels remind us that another popular theme was the flower composition. Bunches and bundles of flowers were often arranged within a circle. These circular pieces were obviously intended to be set in miniature frames covered with a glass shade, and worn like a pendant around the neck. Some may also have graced the tops of snuff or tobacco boxes and been covered with a glass. Cutwork borders for pictures were in use. Often the picture was a religious miniature on vellum, and no doubt many of these paper cuts originated in convents. In France, and perhaps in Germany as well, paper cutting was taught to girls along with calligraphy and painting miniatures. Works of this sort would be preserved in convents and churches with religious veneration and because convents do not move house, and have no very small children about the place, many of these religiously inspired paper cuts have survived. The best collection of *canivets* ever amassed, that of the late Gabriel Magnien, is predominantly religious in tone. Cutwork borders for religious pictures were made in countries other than France. In the museum at Linz there is a miniature painting on vellum of the Flight into Egypt. In the cutwork border an eagle and other birds, stags, and hounds appear amid vine tendrils. Sometimes a picture is all cutwork, such as an example, also at Linz, which shows angels and trophies surrounding a figure of Justice. The composition is dedicated to the State

---

[8.] Ibid., p. 8.

Corner of a parchment Jewish marriage contract, made in Italy in the eighteenth century, ornamented with cutwork and paintings. PHOTOGRAPH BY STELLA MAYES REED.

Deputation of the Province of Nymwegen.

The eighteenth century saw the arrival of new forms of paper work decoration or the consolidation of old ones. In Switzerand the legal document, which we last noticed as receiving ornamentation from Jewish artists in the shape of the vellum or paper *ketubbot*, or marriage contract, came to be particularly important. There is no great similarity of style between Jewish and Swiss cutwork, even if Jewish paper cutting is being carried out in a country near to Switzerland, such as Italy, and is comparable in date. A Jewish marriage contract, drawn up in Verona in 1780, is decorated by painted figures in costume which stand between irregularly shaped medallions, figuring Old Testament scenes. The only motif in the contract which might appear in Swiss work is that of a vase of flowers. Swiss legal documents were likely to be ornamented by elaborate shields, sometimes embellished with interior cutting stuck to the covers of documents. Elaborate borders also ornamented birth certificates, wills, and other formal documents, such as balance sheets. Quite different treatment was given to religious paper cuts in Switzerland. An eightfold cut, made in Grison and dated 1778, incorporates religious maxims, written in formal Gothic black letter, flowering painting, and intertwining scrolls carrying the written legends which remind us of the scrolls on the Runic Stones of Sweden.

Ornamented Swiss legal documents were the work of a professional scrivener, who probably regarded paper cutting as an extension of his skill as a calligrapher. As the eighteenth century went on, however, more and more paper cutting was undertaken, just for amusement, by folk artist of all social classes. In America, where the paper cut had now spread, beautiful découpage of formal gardens with trellis, arbors, and neatly trimmed trees, the whole enclosed in a lacy border, was made by German settlers in Lancaster, Pennsylvania.

In England, whole families seem to have been paper cutters. This at least is what one might assume from the survival of a group of paper cuts, all made by the now extinct family of Ithell, who used to live at Temple Dinsley, Hertfordshire, England. One of the paper cuts is a

Paper cut by Hans Christian Andersen. The bottom right-hand corner has been torn off by accident. In this cut one can find goblins, witches, elves, and other subjects taken from the great Danish writer's fairy tales. The center is symmetrical, the result of a four-fold cut, but the top and bottom halves, made from a double, have each been given a slightly different treatment. PHOTOGRAPH RY STELLA MAYES REED.

Paper cut by Hans Christian Andersen. PHOTOGRAPH BY STELLA MAYES REED.

Shadow Theatre cutout figures of Mameluke emirs, made of camel hide.
PHOTOGRAPH BY STELLA MAYES REED.

*Heraldic and ornamental panel in cut paper. In the center is a coat of arms;
on a bend the three roses; on the crest a dove with an olive branch. Alle-
gorical symbols, such as a pelican in her piety, fill the borders. At the bottom, Abundance holds a cornucopia. An English* canivet *of the early eighteenth century (dated 1725).* COURTESY VICTORIA AND ALBERT MUSEUM,
LONDON.

religious one. It illustrates the story of Jacob's Ladder. Jacob, dressed in formal eighteenth-century garb, is shown pouring a libation in an orchard. Little angels run up and down his ladder. On the right of the paper cut is a poem, with all the letters cut out, not written, like the *Liber Passionis*. The paper cut is backed with green silk. Another beautiful cut of two girls in an orchard, with the two halves of the picture symmetrically disposed, belonged to the same family. Finally, there is a New Year's Greeting card (a new genre) from G. J. K. to Mary Ithell, for 1722. Backed with light purple paper, this cutting shows Cupid tumbling headlong through the sky, down to where Mary sits by her fireside writing at a table, with her cat watching her. Outside in the garden, a squirrel and birds perch on the roof or in the trees.

Another characteristic eighteenth-century form of paper cutting must be noticed. Memorial cuts acted as a perpetual reminder of some lost loved one, like a mourning ring. They were usually the work of folk artists rather than professionals, and often of people of a modest station in life. One beautiful memorial paper cutting, made in blue paper and ornamented with spangles, was dedicated by her grieving husband to Rebecca Woods, who died in 1795. The memorial cut is adorned with verse (written in rather halting grammar and spelling) and with emblems such as urns and weeping willows, framed between flaunting peacocks, bunches of grapes, cupids, and exquisitely fine trelliswork.

The religious cutout continued to be popular throughout the eighteenth century. I must differ from Mr. Basil Long, who feels that the example of *The Creed*, which I illustrate, and which dates from the late eighteenth century, has "a professional touch."[9] To my mind, this work is pure folk art, though it does in fact parallel one of the regular items in the professional's repertoire. Mrs. Seymour, a professional paper artist, exhibited several pieces at the Free Society of Artists between 1765 and 1766. They included: "a frame of various devices, cut in vellum with scissors, containing the Lord's Prayer, with her name, and date of the month and year, in the compass of a silver threepence."[10]

A very favored form of the paper cut was the picture composition, which has already been referred to several times. A landscape with houses and a bridge was "cut with scissors by Miss Mary Holland, Born on the Pedlar's Acre, March 7, 1770, before she was ten years old." This inscription was proudly added to the paper cut by Mrs. Mary Ann Davis, Mary Holland's mother-in-law.

[9.] Basil S. Long, *Antiques* (February 1931), p. 121.

[10.] Magnien, *Canivets, Découpures and Silhouettes.*

Spanish cut paper work of the late eighteenth century. A watercolor portrait on vellum of St. Gregory, or some other saint, framed by a design of birds, flowers, and shepherds with a lamb. COURTESY VICTORIA AND ALBERT MUSEUM, LONDON.

So as to help the amateur in her work, new tools were devised. In a letter addressed to the Marquise de M., and published in the French paper *Mercure* of December 1727, Constantin remarks: "In order to cut paper at first one only used ordinary scissors, afterwards more delicate scissors were employed, for hand cutting, but I have had made scissors which are pointed, thin, and rounded into a sickle shape on the side, and I have had several other tools made, with which one can cut out paper, on a little plank of smooth wood, or of lead which has been softened and prepared. Some are different kinds of punches, a little like those which the pantry servants use to cut out the papers with which they decorate the bowls of fruits and preserves. Other tools are round, pointed, shaped like a hussar's sabre, or like a small crescent. In order to use the punches one employs a little boxwood hammer."[11]

Constantin also gives directions as to what to do with découpage, once it is finished. "When you have cut out the number of pieces necessary for the composition of the subject you want to represent, take as a background cloth, satin, or thin cardboard. Smear this background with a fine and transparent gum. The coat of transparent varnish applied as a finishing touch settles the background into the same attractively even tone."

Constantin mentions the decoration of food by paper cuts. This has continued till our own day, and is an example of unobtrusive art in everyday life. Paper frills still adorn joints of meat in butcher's shops in fashionable London streets. French crystallized fruit still arrives in boxes decorated with perforated paper, though nowadays the paper is decorated by the embossing machine.

If they ever came into general use, the tools which Constantin describes had been superseded, by the nineteenth century, by special kinds of scissors. These had sharp, acute points, and the blades were much shorter than the shanks. Well-rounded, roomy openings were made in the handles for finger and thumb. A special kind of knife, called a "matt knife," later came to be employed for knife cutting. After the steel-nibbed pen came into use in the nineteenth century, penknives were rarely carried except by schoolboys.

Not much is known about how eighteenth-century folk artists set to work. In 1787, just before the French Revolutoin, a nun at Cambray was still cutting out achievements of arms, ornamented by lace patterns, such as *oeil de perdix*. Probably she had graduated to paper cutting by working lace, and she was inspired by the local designs of the province.

11. Ibid.

A much better-known Cambray folk artist was a man called Cadet Rousselle. He was a contemporary of the anonymous nun and worked during the last years of Louis XVI's reign. After his stay in Cambray, he moved to Douai, where he set up a stall in the porch of the church of St. Pierre, around 1809. Here he sold charming paper cuts which were mounted on blue or black paper. He became such a well-known local character that his portrait was painted by two artists of the place.

A visitor to Cambray had described him at work: "There was a poor

The Lord's Prayer within a wreath, enclosed in an ornamental rectangle. Inscribed in ink on the back: "cut by T. Hunter, 1786." COURTESY VICTORIA AND ALBERT MUSEUM, LONDON.

Ann Bancroft Thorneley, 1794-1863. Flowers in a vase. COURTESY VICTORIA
AND ALBERT MUSEUM, LONDON.

devil, weak in the head, at Cambray at this time. He possessed a particular art and skill in cutting out, from a piece of paper placed on a small
board . . . the sort of birds one dreams of, unheard of flowers, and imagi-
nary buildings . . . marvels of patience, skill, and delicacy which one
could only compare to lace.

"The poor wretch could be seen, every morning, installing himself on an
old chair. He was tall, and badly clothed in a russet grey great coat, with
a three-cornered hat battered out of shape as his only headgear [that is,
he did not wear a wig, which was eccentric at this era: *author*]. He held
this hat almost always under his arm and under the other he had a port-
folio containing his masterpieces."[12]

Invariably folk art inspires the demand for something with a more
professional finish to it. Professional artists in paper existed in eighteenth-
century Paris. Le Sieur Bresson de Maillard was an example. In his shop
in the Rue Saint Jacques, he "cut out pictures and designs which ladies
were accustomed to stick onto their screens, lamp shades, boxes, coffers,

[12.] Anonymous, *Canivets De La Collection Gabriel Magnien* Lyons: (Lescuyers & fils).

Panel of cut paper representing Britannia holding the portrait of Frederick, Prince of Wales (George III's father. He never succeeded to the throne because he died after an accident on the cricket field). Nathaniel Bermingham.
COURTESY VICTORIA AND ALBERT MUSEUM, LONDON.

and furniture."[13] He also published a catalogue giving details of his products.

England appears to have been the real home of the professional *découpeur*, however. Prominent among them was Nathaniel Berming-ham: "a most ugly, squinting, mean-looking fellow," who had been apprenticed in his youth to a heraldic painter in Dublin. In *Mortimer's Universal Director* of 1763, he is described as: "Herald Painter and im-prover of the curious art of cutting out Portraits, and Coats of Arms in Vellum, with the point of a penknife . . . Specimens of his peculiar talent may be seen at his house, the corner of Great Queen St., opposite Long Acre." In 1774 he exhibited at the Society of Artists a portrait of the *Duke of Gloucester*, cut in paper in an entirely new manner, along with other compositions probably made in the same way. Bermingham was famous for his portraits, and I illustrate one which I have found and venture to attribute to him, a paper cut of Britannia holding up a portrait of Frederick, Prince of Wales, father of George III, who was himself to take such an interest in paper work.

Mrs. Seymour, who has been already mentioned, also made portraits, including "a head of the King of Poland cut in vellum." She also cut landscapes and animal portraits such as "a squirrel with a nut bough," together with coats or arms and ciphers.

Other professionals working in England included Mrs. Anne Gouyn, who cut "two pieces of flowers, cut in card," and P. L. De la Vega, a Spaniard, who exhibited in 1775 "the portraits of His Majesty and the Princess Royal with the inscription, the whole cut in paper with scissors," together with a portrait, made in the same way, of the Duchess of Gor-don. The panache of A. Chearnly, who created a bust of Cicero entirely from connected openwork flourishes in 1744, suggests that he must have been a professional.

By the opening of the nineteenth century, professional artists had become much less conspicuous; the field was left to amateurs and folk artists. A few professionals continued to dabble in paper cutting. In Dusseldorf, Germany, William Muller (1804-65) cut delightful land-scapes, with goats perched on rocky crags, and scenes of peasant life. Philip Otto Runge (1777-1810), another German paper cutter, became much more famous on account of his paintings, but he continued to make cuts of animals, flowers, trees, and landscapes, often cutting them out during his country walks. These compositions he gave away to his friends.

[13.] Article in *The Times*, January 15, 1966.

W. J. Hubard, the American silhouette artist, made paper cuts as well. The boy prodigy's advertisement informed his patrons that he was prepared to supply them with "Perspective Views, Architectural, Military, and Sporting Pieces."

Another professional paper cutter, also a silhouettist, was at work in the Crystal Palace during the Great Exhibition of 1851. *The Expositor* of July 26th, 1851, noted: "Some beautiful specimens of cutting in paper, in imitation of nature, have recently been placed on the walls of the staircase [at the Crystal Palace: *author*]. They are the productions of Mr. F. Windsor, the profile artist at the Royal Polytechnic Institution. They consist of a cedar tree and landscape, an elm tree in high relief, a landscape and an imitation of an etching. They are of a large size, one being 2 ft. 10 in. by 3 ft."

Hubbard employed the folded paper cut, in which both halves of a composition are cut at once, for his dream-like pictures of oriental gardens. Much more to the taste of the English public during the 1820s were the same artist's *Scenes of Dr. Syntax*, a subject taken from a satirical poem. These cutouts, which could easily be classed as either découpage or silhouette, were groups of figures cut from black paper and pasted onto a quickly sketched color wash background.

Other English professionals working between 1820 and 1830 advertised paper cuts which could be stuck into ladies' albums. The subjects included landscapes, seascapes, animals, group of flowers, and pictorial compositions. Amateurs made the same kind of paper cuts and gave them to their friends as presents, which they would treasure in scrap books bound in blue or red morocco leather, with colored paper leaves, and closed with a silver lock.

Découpage continued to be a very popular pastime among English amateurs, as well as their European counterparts. "In the early part of the present century," wrote S. J. Houslen in 1896, "the cutting out of figures from paper with scissors still formed one of the common evening diversions of young people, though the subjects chosen by the humble amateur did not often rise above the difficulties of still life, household furniture, chairs, tables and so forth. Sometimes a performer of more than ordinary skill would attack domestic animals, carriages, and horses, and dancing figures, while one of higher aspirations still might attempt to represent a panoramic landscape."[14]

A whole book of cuttings was made by an amateur called Mrs. R. Hughes, at the age of 71, around the middle of the nineteenth century.

14. S.J. Housley, "Shadows of the Great," *Strand Magazine* (1896).

When completed it was presented to "her dear daughter, Mrs. Frederick Gyd." Mrs. Hughes cut delicate flower groups in black paper.

At about the same time the Townshend family were working on shadow cuttings. These were portraits in which the white parts of the portrait were cut out. When they were held up to a strong light and their shadow fell on a piece of paper it looked like a black and white portrait.

The album was one of the great outlets of the amateur cutter. Elizabeth, daughter of George III, had kept her cuttings in a blue morocco album. Queen Victoria also had an album in which she kept her collection of paper work. By the nineteenth century the album had become sentimental as well as just artistic. Eighteenth-century amateurs had sent loving paper cuts to their sweethearts. During the nineteenth century, young men of artistic ability turned their attention to the paper cut Valentine. Valentines were made to open to reveal a complete wedding trousseau cut out of white paper—rather daring in its attention to detail. Other Valentines were envelopes which contained white paper gloves— real white gloves were always worn at weddings. Others frothed with cut lacework, and opened their trellis doors to reveal "bestuck and bleeding hearts," floral arrangements and cupids. They made use of many devices, such as Leander swimming the Hellespont to see his mistress, and employed motifs which sometimes appear in other countries, such as the endless knot, which also appeared in sentimental paper cutting in Switzerland. Real artistry was shown both in the amateur and professionally made Valentine, but the demand was so great that mass production began to prevail over artistry. By 1824, when Dobbs and Co. of London began manufacturing Valentines, the embossing machine had been invented. Paper lace could now be mass-produced by means of rollers, or by a screw press that made use of brass dies. Borders of mechanically cut paper work were small at first, but soon covered almost the whole of the Valentine. The border became just as important as the picture or design which it enclosed. Valentine firms ordered lace paper by the ton, and cut paper became not a delicate, handmade art, but just another item of machine-made decoration.

Although the embossing machine had destroyed most people's interest in handmade lacy paper designs of the *canivet* school, one or two local schools of paper cutting continued to survive in Europe throughout the nineteenth century.

An interesting example is Jewish paper cutting, an art permeated with religious, if not magical lore. Nineteenth-century Jewish paper cuts were double-folded, nailed lightly down to a wooden board and cut with a knife. They might then be tinted in water color and adorned with Hebrew calligraphy. Motifs which occur in Jewish art keep on popping up in the paper work of other countries. Cavalrymen, beloved of Talmudic scribes, figure largely in the work of the Swiss folk artist, Hauswirth, whose paper cuts will be discussed in a moment. The Jewish paper cuts called *Shiviti* and *Royselek* were stuck to the windows of houses during the holiday of *Shavuot*. Anyone could have seen them, admired them, and decided to copy them, just as the Jewish paper artists themselves may have received their original inspiration from encountering a Turkish bride with her face ornamented with gold paper cutouts. In the Middle East, special paper cuts mounted with metal foil were made. They feature the seven-branched candlestick and often embody Eastern motifs, such as the silhouette hand. In the Middle East, Africa, and Europe, paper cuts were used either as charms (to hasten childbirth, for example) or to mark the eastern wall of the synagogue, toward which prayer should be directed. These were called *Mizrah*, and are the equivalent of the eastern marker point in a mosque, called a *methrab*. One typical *Mizrah*, made in Galicia in 1875, contains a seven-branched candlestick, pillars up which cats try to clamber, winged griffins, deer, eagles, doves and the tree of life. Another example, from twentieth century Poland this time, contains the Ten Commandments, pillars, lions, birds, and foliage. Paper cuts of this sort were widely spread among Jewish communities in Poland (where there was also a lively local school of paper cutting, which is noticed elsewhere), Russia and Germany.

The Swiss, too, clung to their paper cuts. In the eighteenth century, as has already been noticed, the Swiss paper artists had devised all sorts of attractive shapes, including endless woven bands, stars, shields topped with crowns with outer frets and interior embellishment, and eight folded borders, adorned with religious maxims or seasonal good wishes in black letter calligraphy. They had developed paper cuts to ornament furniture, as well as legal documents, love letters, religious texts, and New Year's cards. In the nineteenth century a gifted school of pictorial paper cutters developed, of whom three at least are known by name. Johann Jakob Hauswirth (1807-71), the most eminent of the three, was born at Saanen, in the Pays d'Enhaut of the Vaudois. He was better known to his countrymen by his nickname—*le grand des Marques*, ("the big man with the paper cuts") than by his real name. In Switzerland the paper cut had retained the name of *marque* from the time during the sixteenth century when the smaller kind of découpage compositions had served as bookmarks. Hauswirth was a tall man with a straggling gait, which made children yell "Three Pieces," after him in the street because he almost seemed to be coming apart as he shambled along. He had enormous hands, and such large fingers that he was forced to fit special loops into the scissors he used for cutting paper so as to be able to hold them properly.

Johann worked as a charcoal burner and woodcutter on Radomont mountain, to the north of Rougemont. He had built a cottage for himself in the forest of Des Gorges du Pissot, the most inaccessible part of the Vaudois. In the morning he would leave for his work in the forest, returning at evening, when he would settle down at the kitchen table, reach for the satchel in which he kept his scissors and his *papier de caramel*, and begin work on his paper cuts. *Papier de caramel* was a kind of paper in which shopkeepers used to make the cornets or twists of paper in which they sold candy to children. Johann also used variegated paper, printed paper and flowered paper for his collage compositions, but here we are concerned with his plain paper cuts. William Muller, the German paper cutter who was mentioned earlier, whose life overlaps Hauswirth's, and whose work may have influenced the Swiss artist, usually built up his paper cuts with one layer of action displayed above another. Hauswirth did the same. He usually constructed his paper composition by making a double fold, with two symmetrical sides, often formed by a woman with a parasol, or a horseman blowing a trumpet, on either side of a large center motif. A favorite ingredients for his paper cuts were a vase of flowers (copied perhaps from a printer's flowered capital letter). Often Hauswirth would "sign" this flower vase by cutting on it the Bear of Berne, which was a trademark of his. Apart from this bear signature he never signed his work, and if any initials appear on his paper cuts they are those of the patron at whose commission the cut was made. Johann employed several types of flowers, including the carnation and centaury, and also frequently used a heart as a center motif. Within the heart two bounding chamois or stags might appear. Birds, cows wearing cowbells, fir trees, and cavalrymen on prancing horses are other characteristic Hauswirth decorations.

Le grand des marques, though an ignorant peasant whose outspoken sallies shocked, when they did not amuse, Swiss and foreign tourists, had a real sense of style. His compositions always balanced up and he was never lacking in invention to fill in the corners and blank spaces. Everything in his arrangements was made subordinate to the whole design, even if it meant that there was just one flower in a garden, and that flower out-topped the garden hedge. Everything had a symbolic meaning. The single flower stood for the whole of nature. Many of the ideas for Johann's paper cuts appear in the work of other cultures—for example, trees are widely used in Polish paper work, while prancing cavalrymen appear in Jewish paper cuts. As cut by Johann, however, all these motifs had a very local flavor, and because most of his ideas were interpreted through his experience of his native Vaudois, his work possesses a strength and validity denied to other, more derivative artists.

When he was working, not for a commission but on speculation, Johann would carry round with him his stock of *marques* on long journeys from Etiraz to Lauenen. In the small towns in which he stopped on the way, such as Moulins, Chateau d'Oex, Flendruz, Rougemont, and Gessenay, he would go from house to house, selling his paper cuts to the peasants or to English holiday makers. Many of them are still treasured in the farmhouses of the Vaudois as heirlooms from which the owners would not be parted at any price.

Luois Sangy (1871-1953) was a fitting successor to Hauswirth, as was Christian Schwizgebel (born 1914) who is famous for his beautiful flower pieces in heart-shaped frames. At the end of the line comes Christian Rubi of Berne, who is not merely a paper artist of genius, but a fine teacher who has tried to keep découpage alive as a living folk art in Switzerland.

Paper cutting has never quite disappeared as a living art, though the Joanna Koertens have disappeared with the patrons like the Emperor Rudolph, whose interest and support helped them to perfect their art. Hubert Leslie, who combined silhouettes with landscape and flower paper cuts, illustrated books with the medium revived by him, and wrote an instructive work on *Silhouettes and Scissor Cutting*. He gave an exhibition of his original scissor cuts in 1932 on which occasion the late Queen Mary, the Queen Mother, purchased one of his compositions, *Wistaria*. This was probably the last acquisition, by a sovereign, of the work of a contemporary paper cutter.

5

Rolled Paper or Filigree

ROLLED paper work or filigree, as it is often called, is perhaps the most interesting, and certainly the least well documented of all the paper arts. Like pin-prick, the art has died out completely, although it was practiced until comparatively modern times. In its heyday, which was between 1640 and 1800, rolled paper was made by rolling strips of paper into spirals, and gluing them onto a shallow box frame, while pinning them until the glue had set. The paper was colored and gilded, and an almost infinite number of prefabricated shapes were evolved that could play their part in the finished design, including rolls, volutes, spirals, cones, and watch-spring shapes. The individual units formed in this way were built up into a very elaborate design, which usually took thousands of pieces of paper to complete. The box in which the rolled paper designs were arranged was often lined with white silk or some similar showy background, and the completed composition was framed like a picture. Rolled paper was also frequently used for the decoration of furniture, from small-sized pieces such as tea caddies to harpsichord cases, screens, and cabinets.

Just as paper cutting originated from designs cut on parchment with a *canivet*, so rolled paper work was apparently preceded by rolled strips of parchment, which were gilded to represent gilt metal filigree, and used to ornament reliquaries and other religious accessories in the monasteries and convents of pre- Reformation England.

Filigree, or rolled paper work, underwent a revival toward the middle of the seventeenth century. The diarist, Samuel Pepys, makes a reference,

Rolled-paper tea caddies made by French prisoners of war. COURTESY LONDON
MUSEUM.

on May 4th, 1663, to a piece which is almost certainly a work in rolled
paper: "This day I received a baskett from my sister Pall, made by her
of paper, which hath a great deal of labour in it for country innocent
work."[1] Thereafter, literary references to rolled paper, or mosaic, become more frequent in the court circle of James II's Queen, Mary of
Modena. In a letter to Lady Margaret Russell, then a Lady in Waiting,
the writer comments: "In gum flowers, Mrs. Booth tells me you and she
is to do something in that work, which I suppose must be extraordinary."[2]
Rolled paper may have been carried by the Stuart court from London
to St. Germains, where James II and his family went into exile. At all
events, it was well established in French convents by the eighteenth century, and the author of the article in the *Encyclopaedie* which deals with
it remarks: "Paper gilded with gold leaf made of fine gold serves to
adorn reliquaries, little devotional pictures, and other little works. Nuns
employ, for the same work, silvered paper, and cardboard which is
gilded on the edge, made up into little strips with which they carry out
all these little gilded spirals which are in the reliquaries. These papers,
as much gilded as silvered, as well as cardboard gilt on the edge, are
made in Paris."[3]
Much of this fine convent work still survives in the collection of the
late Gilbert Magnien, which is now at Lyons Museum in France. Other
examples have found their way to England. Attractive examples in the

[1]. Richard Lord Braybrooke, ed., *The Diary of Samuel Pepys* (Lonon: Frederick Warne.
1887).
[2]. Hannah Robertson, *Life* (Birmingham: 1791).
[3]. G. Magnien, *Canivets, Découpures and Silhouettes* (Lyons, 1947), p. 16.

London Museum, Kensington Palace, London, include a panel of eighteenth or late seventeenth-century work in which delicately restrained volutes and spirals surround an engraving of St. John, which has been cut out, framed in paper, and hand colored. Another convent example, preserved in the same museum, is an eighteenth-century reliquary having for its centerpiece a wax medallion bearing the imprint of the Paschal Lamb.

In England, one of the principal uses of rolled paper work was to compose family coats of arms. Fine works of this sort have been preserved at the London Museum. They include a panel, dating from about 1700, bearing the arms of the family of Lawson- Tancred of Adborough and Boroughbridge, Yorkshire, a coat of arms of Cooke impaling Osbourne, with elaborate mantling and border, and a shield of arms of an unknown family bearing "two luces haurient," joined by a ribbon, with elaborate mantling and swags of flowers.

A very fine panel of the Royal Arms of George I is preserved in the Victoria and Albert Museum, London, England. In this panel, which is possibly the most ambitious piece of rolled paper work ever devised, the heraldic beasts, the crest, and the mantling, are all of rolled paper work that has been coaxed from its normal flattened position into a three-dimensional sculpture. Crescent-shaped swags suggest that this shield is technically allied to other contemporary work in the London Museum.

The shield of arms was, of all types of rolled paper work, the longest lasting. One coat of arms, with the monogram "V.I.R." ("Victoria Empress and Queen"), which was constructed from rolled paper in gold on a purple background, with flowers to match, was placed by the sarcophagus at Frogmore, on the funeral of Queen Victoria on February 1st, 1901. This shield must have been made after 1876, when Victoria took the title "Empress and Queen" by the Royal Titles Act. It was preserved by Lord Pelham Clinton, Master of the Household to the Queen.

Models of houses were another outlet for the rolled-paper worker. A good example, portraying a Queen Anne house, is to be found in the London Museum. Portraits were another favored kind of work. Wisely, the craftswomen did not attempt to make the bust, or face, of the portrait in paper. This kind of three-dimensional shaping had achieved success with the modeling of the heraldic beasts in the George I coat of arms, where an element of the grotesque helped the modeler. It would have been too ambitious, however, to attempt this technique in the portrait of a human being. Instead, the portraitist substituted the head and bust of a wax doll for the portrait proper, and concentrated on gorgeous

Italian rolled-paper panel in gilt and colors, framing a small painted print of St. John. Probably eighteenth century. COURTESY LONDON MUSEUM.

robes and surroundings of princely magnificence for the rolled-paper work.

Charming examples of portraits of this sort include a panel in the Lady Lever Collection, Port Sunlight, Cheshire, England, dated 1702, in which the head and shoulders of a girl doll look out through an oval window surrounded by swags, garlands, birds, vases of flowers, and an elaborate border. In another example from the same collection, a very regal Queen Anne stands between draped columns. Two more portraits of monarchs, one of which portrays William and Mary, are to be found in the London Museum.

In the early years of the eighteenth century, rolled-paper work underwent something of a decline; then, toward the end of the century, it began to revive. "At York," notes Hannah Robertson, "I found employment in the boarding schools, particularly in the line of filigree, which, from having been long neglected, appeared like a new art."[4] In fact, filigree became one of the regular occupations recommended to young

4. Robertson, *Life*.

Rolled-paper model of a house front of the Queen Anne period. COURTESY
LONDON MUSEUM.

ladies to keep them out of mischief, such as reading novels, for example.
"Our great-grandmothers," wrote Maria Edgeworth at the end of the
eighteenth century, "distinguished themselves by truly substantial tent-
stitch chairs and tables, by needlework pictures of Solomon and his
queen, Sheba, that were so admirable in their day, but their day is now
over. Filigree baskets take their place instead."[5]

Maria Holroyd, a young girl from Sheffield Place, Sussex, England,
commented in 1786: "I have learnt the Filigree work for this winter,
and have done a box in purple, green, and gold for mama. It is dirty
work, the dye of the paper comes off when wet with gum."[6]

Professional paper filigree workers taught leisured amateurs, such as
schoolgirls, and sold their finished work. "I therefore took a house,"
wrote Hannah Robertson, the most famous professional, "and with my
daughters, Minia opened a shop (the first of its kind in London) for
various works of fancy; and here, Madam, I might have made a second
fortune; our shop was crowded with nobility, and we were also employed
in teaching many of the first families.

[5] Robertson, *Life*.
[6] Quoted by Bea Howe in the article "Parlour Accomplishments," *Country Life*
(December 10, 1948).

*Heraldic panel of rolled paper, with a coat of arms of two "luces haurient,"
joined by a ribbon, with elaborate mantling, swags of flowers above with
cones and scroll borders, and a silk background.* **COURTESY LONDON MUSEUM.**

Heraldic panel of rolled paper, displaying the arms of Lawson Tancred of Aldborough and Boroughbridge in Yorkshire. COURTESY LONDON MUSEUM.

"His grace the Duke of———made us known to Lady Charlotte Finch, who sent for my daughter to instruct the Princess; but there were some reasons which induced her to decline the honour that was offered her. Windsor Castle, however, is now ornamented with a great variety of this kind of works."[7]

Though Hannah Robertson's daughter, Minia, did not teach George III's girls to make rolled-paper work, they learned it from Mrs. Delany, and Princess Elizabeth became as dedicated an enthusiast for filigree as she was for other paper crafts. Charles Elliott, the purveyor of artist's materials to the royal family, supplied her "with fifteen ounces of different filigree papers, one ounce of gold paper, and a box made for filigree-work with ebony moulding, lock, and key, lined inside and outside with a tea cadde '(caddy')' to correspond with the box."[8]

Amateurs like Princess Elizabeth who were looking for patterns for filigree work could find them in women's journals such as *The New Lady Magazine* which between 1786 and 1787 issued no fewer than twelve pattern sheets for filigree, engraved and designed by Stuart. *The Lady's Magazine* for 1786 also printed four pattern illustrations.

Tea caddies (boxes for holding tea, which was taxed so heavily in England that it had to be locked up in a special container, for fear the servants should steal it) were a favorite subject for rolled-paper decoration at the end of the century. *The Gentleman's Magazine* for 1791 comments on how popular a pastime this has become among ladies. The ready-made boxes were bought from a cabinet maker. They were square, or octagonal in shape. Their side panels, which were later to be covered with rolled-paper designs, were made of soft wood, which would best hold the pins. Parts of the caddy which would not be covered by the finished design were made from rosewood, ebony, or ivory, smoothed and polished. Sometimes they were enriched with marquetry, and ornamented with a knob to lift the lid, an interior lid to help keep the tea fresh and a silver lock and key.

Tea caddies, decorated with rolled-paper work, were made in the prison camps by French prisoners of war during the Napoleonic wars, and probably by American prisoners as well. The prisoners also made beautiful compositions of paper flowers, in which roses, sweet peas, and passion flowers rose in graceful groups from baskets. Good examples of tea caddies were made by French prisoners at Falmouth, and Normans Cross. Fine specimens can also be seen in the Arthur R. Sawyer collec-

7. Robertson, *Life.*
8. Bernard Hughes, "English Filigree Paper Work," *Country Life,* (September 21, 1951).

Heraldic shield of rolled-paper work, showing the arms of Cooke impaling Osbourne, with elaborate mantling and border. COURTESY LONDON MUSEUM.

tion in Chicago. More will be said about the techniques of making rolled paper later, but it may be mentioned here that the prisoners built up their work by applying many tiny strips of paper, an eighth of an inch wide, either colored or gilt-edged, to the blank recess of a caddy with veneered flanges. The paper strips were wound into coiled figures with the gilt edge outward, and glued to the plain deal backing. Any spaces left between the elegantly convoluting strips were filled in with tightly rolled paper coils. Sometimes the background was filled in with metal foil paper, cut into patterns, such as leaves. The appearances of these French rolled-paper caddies has been compared to *cloisonné* enamel, or mother-of-pearl carving. Attractive though they are, we certainly cannot see them now as they appeared when they left the prisoners' workshops. A tea caddy is an article of furniture which is likely to get a good deal of use in an English home, and years of sunlight have faded the brightly colored paper to the gentlest of pastel tones.

Not only tea caddies, but large items of furniture were ornamented with rolled paper as well. A cabinet in the Lady Lever Art Gallery, is decorated with rolled-paper designs which must have required months, if not years, to complete. It has fourteen drawers and a cupboard, all ornamented with rolled paper. Table tops, fire screens, trays, ink stands, and picture frames were also decorated in this way.

By one of the ironies of history, we know more about one of the professional rolled-paper workers of the eighteenth century than we do about any of the famous amateurs—even George III's daughter, Princess Elizabeth, because Hannah Robertson, besides writing on instructional text book on rolled paper and other paper crafts, left a long biographical memoir, or rather a printed begging letter, intended to move the compassionate to contribute to her distress. Even in an age which had raised the begging letter to a fine art, Mrs. Robertson's readers must have been touched merely by the title page of her "Life," which was dated from Birmingham, October 15th, 1791.

"The Life of Mrs. Robertson, (A Tale of Truth as well as of Sorrow) Who, Though a Grand Daughter of Charles II, Has Been Reduced, By A Variety Of Very Uncommon Events, From Splendid Affluence to the greatest Poverty, And, After Having Buried Nine Children, Is Obliged, At The Age of Sixty-Seven, To earn a scanty Maintenance for herself and two Orphan Grand Children, By Teaching Embroidery, Filigree, and the Art of making Artificial Flowers.

"I am a Grand Daughter of King Charles IId," Hannah began. "My father was born in Windsor castle, towards the close of the reign of that Prince, his mother being a daughter of the D———family, a name too

Rolled-paper heraldic panel, showing the coat of arms of an unidentified family. COURTESY LONDON MUSEUM.

much distinguished to appear in the same narrative with mine; but which in confidence (were it required) I should not object to reveal."[9]

While still a babe in arms, the Merry Monarch's love child was handed over to the care of the wife of a gunner at the Castle of Windsor. The gunner's wife, who was called Swan, had the baby baptized in her own name. A little older, the boy was handed over to a Mr. Gibson, the Master of the Mint in Edinburgh, to be brought up. When he was grown, Swan married an heiress called Ramsay. When his first wife died he remarried and had Hannah, among other children. Swan's royal blood was recognized by the Scots nobility. "I have been told," said Hannah "that the Dutchess of Hamilton, after her lord had lost his head, would never permit more than one chair to be in her room, lest anyone should sit down in her presence, but when my father visited her, she called for a second to do honour to the blood in his veins."

Her father had been quite an old man when he married for the second

9. Robertson, *Life.*

*Rolled-paper heraldic shield of an unidentified family. Second half of the
seventeenth century.* COURTESY VICTORIA AND ALBERT MUSEUM, LONDON.

time, and when he died his widow, in her turn, married again, this time
Alexander Christie, a prosperous linen manufacturer. "I was too proud,"
she tells her readers, "to join the children of a little neighbouring school,
to which I was ordered to go. I retired unseen to a closet, which I called
my own, laid out the little money I could get in paint and paper, and
thus early and without any mistress, but kind nature, began to practise

myself in embroidery, drawing, making flowers, and various other ele-
gant works of fancy; arts which ever after continued the amusements of
my leisure in prosperity, and to which I am indebted for an unfailing
resource, during a long and painful series of adverse fortune."

Her stepfather, who had bought a splendid estate in the Highlands
of Scotland in Perthshire, near to his linen manufactory, surrounded
her with every luxury. For some time she lived a life of idyllic happiness, until her stepfather, "possessing a depraved inclination, and a
vulgar mind, felt no pleasure but in scenes of dissipation, and folly . . .
frequented those few towns, that were in reach of our retirement, pre-
ferring the rude revelry of riot, to the sacred silence of philosophic
solitude, often returning like a Bacchanal to prophane those scenes
which should have been consecrated to contemplation and to wisdom."

As her family fortunes crumbled, Hannah became involved in a whole
series of romantic and tragic happenings, events more improbable and
affecting than could be found in any novel. A young physician who lived
nearby fell violently in love with Hannah, whom the circumstances of
her life show to have been a girl of extraordinary beauty. She could not
return his affection, and he pined away and died of a broken heart.
"Thus," she writes, "Circumstance preyed upon my mind and that gloomy
cast of features which marks the child of sorrow, began from this time
to be immoveably fixed."

In the year 1744 she found someone whom she could love, a young
officer in one of the English regiments stationed in Scotland, whom she
calls "Mr. B." Though he was a wealthy man, heir to an estate of £8,000
a year, "I am not conscious," she says, "that interest had any share in
fixing my choice, and indeed the alliance of nobility could scarcely have
flattered my vanity, knowing myself to be the grand daughter of a king.

"Everything was now preparing to celebrate my marriage with Mr. B.,
but in this interval his regiment was ordered into Flanders; he was compelled to march at the head of his soldiers—he fought for his country—
and *died* in reinforcing Ghent."

Crushed by this private tragedy, poor Hannah remained unmoved
among the scenes of devastation which took place round her Highland
home as the supporters of Bonny Prince Charlie rose in the '45 Rebel-
lion in an attempt to place their leader on the British throne. "I have
sometimes since thought," she noted in her memoirs, "that to these
scenes of horror I am indebted for a firmness—perhaps a callousness of
mind. At Perth I could sit, and listen to the cannons with stoical apathy,
though it frequently happened that every pane of glass in every window
was demolished in the house where I resided, and a cannon ball once

passed thro' the bed, in an apartment next to that in which I was sleeping."

When the English troops drove back the Jacobite army, from Perthshire to its final defeat at Culloden, Perth was reoccupied by a regiment that numbered in its ranks a Captain Johnstone. Johnstone fell in love with the fair maid of Perth, and wooed her successfully, but as the dates set for their wedding approached, he, too, was ordered to Flanders, just as her first sweetheart had been, to the siege of Bergen op Zoom.

"For some time I often heard from him," wrote Hannah." But soon I heard no more. I counted the slow hours—I watched the winds in vain! News at last came that the siege was over, and that the army was returning, but the next post informed me that the transport on which Captain Johnstone's company had embarked was windbound, then that it had sailed, that in the greatest distress it had reached England, after a tedious voyage of five months, during which time the whole crew had experi-

Panel of rolled paper surrounding the portrait of a child in wax. COURTESY LADY LEVER ART GALLERY, CHESHIRE, ENGLAND, with acknowledgments to the Trustees of The LADY LEVER ART GALLERY, PORT SUNLIGHT.

Rolled-paper picture enclosing the heads in wax of two sovereigns (William and Mary?). COURTESY LONDON MUSEUM.

enced the most complicated misery, and that the two officers who accompanied the men were dead."

At this second fatal blow to her hopes of love and marriage Hannah seems to have given up hope. Her mother, however, began to look around for a husband for her, one who was rich enough to shore up the failing family fortunes. Just such a man was found in the wealthy Mr. Robertson, grandson to "the proudest man in Perth." Unable to support her mother's importunities, Hannah, agreed to marry Robertson. On the eve of her wedding, Johnson returned from the dead! His letters had been intercepted. He had embarked on board the transport, but an unexpected accident had recalled him to land before the vessel sailed, and from that time a strange and even romantic concurrence of unfortunate events had detained him abroad.

For some reason that is not adequately explained, Hannah felt she must go through with the wedding to Robertson. "The fatal morning arrived. I endeavoured to compose my features for the occasion, and suffered myself to be adorned with the ornaments of a bride: I was led (like a victim crowned with garlands) to the altar; renouncing forever the man I loved—and entering into the most solemn engagements to love that man, whom I now considered the fatal cause of unutterable woe."

Robertson, although he was an heir who had not yet come into his full expectations, was a wealthy man. "I remember," wrote Hannah, "to have been almost the first person who possessed at that time, and in that part of the country, an entire tea equipage of plate [silver] with every other suitable accompaniment." A more important acquisition than a silver teapot was the friendship of the Duchess of Athole, who was destined to become a lifelong supporter of Hannah. Then a further blow descended. Captain Johnstone, though thwarted in his hopes of marrying Hannah, had remained her faithful but platonic friend and admirer.

"I was now preparing for a little stranger who was likely to increase our family: one day as I sat musing alone, Captain Johnstone unexpectedly appeared and, falling upon one knee, before me, he put into my hand a splendid coral [a silver mounted coral branch was used by eighteenth-century mothers to enable babies to cut their teeth, like a comforter nowadays] which he begged I would present to the young stranger, whom (he told me) his happiness required he should never behold. Captain Johnstone left the room before I had courage to reply; and although near fifty years have since passed away, I never from that fatal period have once enjoyed the melancholy satisfaction of beholding him more. If my friend (for I dare no longer call him lover [a word which meant merely "suitor" in the eighteenth century]) be yet on earth, may he have regained that peace I have so long outlived! Or if in heaven, may he enjoy there the reward of his constancy, and of his virtues, unconscious of the woes which his fatal affection has entailed on this sad sorrowing heart."

In an attempt to find solace in her unhappy marriage, Hannah wrote: "The short intervals of leisure, which my duties allowed, were chiefly devoted to those favourite arts which I had ever cultivated with delight."

Nothing could restore her happiness, however. Her eldest son, the one whose approaching birth had brought about her separation with Johnstone, died, and for a time Hannah lost her reason. Her husband devoted all his time to nursing her. He neglected his business to spend time by his wife's bedside, with the result that he went bankrupt when his firm was caught up in the crash of an allied house.

The shock of the disaster revived Hannah from her mental stupor. She helped her husband set up a distillery, but he was imprisoned for a small debt. Undaunted, Hannah made her way to Aberdeen with her children and became an innkeeper. She ran the Freemasons' Tavern, and made such a success of it that she was able not only to earn enough money to have her husband released from his debt, but to be charitable to the poor of the city. "And to many a dependant heir," she wrote, "have I administered his daily bread, who at this time is wanting only in the will to requite me. How deceitful are human prospects! A gentleman from Norway who lodged in our house, unhappily falling asleep as he was reading in bed, the curtains took fire, and the flames communicating with other parts of the furniture and buildings, a great share of our possessions were consumed." A second, and even more disastrous fire, forced Hannah to move to Perth, where she tried to keep a school. "Behold, Madam," she wrote, "the grand-child of a king, reduced to the painful necessity of relying for her support upon that class, with which she was formerly too proud to associate." She fell into debt, and was imprisoned.

"They led me into a damp and dismal dungeon; but I cannot say that it was *not inhabited*; for the place was occupied in every part by innumerable *rats*, the only creature that chills me with horror."

She was able to prove that the imprisonment had been an illegal one, but a new catastrophe followed. She was returning home after a visit to her noble friend, the Duchess of Athole, in the Duchess' coach, when the coachman decided to cross the river Almond by driving over the ice of its frozen waters. The ice broke and Hannah was thrown into the freezing waters. On the ride back to Perth she was robbed, and nearly murdered, by a highwayman.

In the midst of all these adventures, Hannah somehow found time to write a handbook on paper craft and other genteel arts, which seems to have had considerable success. "I now printed the *Young Ladies School of Arts*, which, at the request of some female friends of distinction, I had composed at Aberdeen, and went to Edinburgh to inspect the press." She had taken her daughter Anna with her to Edinburgh while she read and corrected the proofs of her book. There Anna met and married Dr. Wilson, "nephew to a physician of that name; a distinguished character: He had travelled through Europe and Asia, and in a visit to China, had been by a variety of strange accidents introduced to the empress, whom he cured of a dangerous disease." Hannah decided to settle in Edinburgh, and in the winter of 1771 her husband set off on foot to join them, from Perth. He wandered off the road: "and the next morning my dear husband was found amid the drifted snow, a stiff and lifeless corse."

To support herself and her family until her son-in-law Wilson succeeded to his expectations, Hannah advertised in the newspapers for

Wax doll and rolled-paper portrait of Queen Anne. COURTESY LADY LEVER
ART GALLERY, CHESHIRE, ENGLAND, with acknowledgments to the Trustees
of The LADY LEVER ART GALLERY, PORT SUNLIGHT.

patrons who wanted to be taught filigree and other paper crafts. "The Duchess of Gordon read the advertisement, and with the consent of her Lord, sent for me to the castle. Here I passed four months." A desire to return to her family finally compelled her to leave Huntly Castle, and she went back to Edinburgh, where she supported herself by "practising and teaching the various arts I understood." Her son-in-law had now inherited the fortune for which he had been waiting so long, but "he had ever possessed a taste for dissipation," wrote Hannah, "and being now possesed also of the means, behold him plunging at once into the tide of fashion and folly." Life at Dr. Wilson's house now became a continual orgy, and in the midst of one wild revel, he even offered his wife, Anna, to one of his boon companions. Anna indignantly refused. A little later, however: "Dr. Wilson, having almost ruined his fortune by a course of boundless extravagance, was now determined to settle in America with the small portion that remained. Alas Madam! Think with what anguish my daughter looked forward to the horror of her situation, conveyed as it were to distant worlds, without a mother, and without a friend!" Rather than face the prospect of emigrating to America with her husband, she decided to live with his friend instead. Unable to bear the disgrace of living near to a daughter who had lapsed from the path of virtue, Hannah moved to York, where her eldest boy was working as an apprentice. As has already been noticed, Hannah sought work by teaching in the boarding schools at York, "but I was often in distress and was compelled to sell the few valuables I had about me." She became so ill that she could not work, and in her poverty her son tried to relieve her by painting and selling Barcelona handkerchiefs, shawls, and kerchiefs.

In spite of the disgrace which Anna had brought on the family, Hannah could not forget about her strayed lamb. She made enquiries, and found that Anna was living in Dublin, having been long ago abandoned by her protector. Hannah sent her the money to come to York, and taught her rolled paper and other paper crafts so that she could support herself respectably. Hitherto Anna had been working as a sercant. "Hardly a vestige of her former self remained," wrote her mother, "she had been obliged to stain her skin with walnut juice, for some families objecting to her beauty, had refused to employ her."

Anna did so well as a teacher of rolled-paper work in Manchester that she persuaded her mother to come and settle in that town. Thence mother and daughter moved to London. There followed a brief period during which Hannah could earn enough to support herself. Then followed the last act of the tragedy. Her beloved Anna died of a lingering disease, another daughter married a midshipman, who went into a decline, and Hannah was left, alone, with two orphan grandchildren to provide for. All the rest of her family were dead, or scattered. "The wealth of nations cannot heal the wounds yet bleeding at my heart . . . Yet Madam, by your interposition, perhaps I yet may pass in peace the future closing scenes of life, whilst one mild gleam of setting light shines on my evening hours."

It is an appeal that might move a heart of stone. Perhaps it did move the heart of Princess Elizabeth, whose hands had made many of the paper ornaments which decorated Windsor Castle, and who had nearly become Anna's pupil.

With the end of Hannah Robertson's romantic history, the artistic period of rolled-paper work well nigh disappears. Cheap and garish seaside souvenirs now began to be produced in the medium. A large workbox of about 1840, now preserved in the London Museum, contains interior compartment boxes ornamented with woolwork and feather mosaic. The rolled paper decorations are made from thin, almost crepe paper. These decorations surround panels of cardboard painted with seaside scenes. This box has nothing to recommend it except historical interest.

Rolled-paper work lingered on for a time. In 1850, Lady Dorothy Nevill described herself as "doing a kind of old fashioned paperwork which consists in arranging little strips of coloured paper into decorative patterns, as was done in the eighteenth century." Some years later, in 1875, W. Bemrose, Jr., wrote a book called *Mosaicon, or Paper Mosaic,* which was a handbook intended to revive the art. His attempt was unsuccessful; some time after the following year, 1876, as has already been noted, the last datable piece of paper work was made. Rolled-paper work is now so completely dead that it has never been revived, even by the forgers, which is more than can be said of many of the other paper arts.

The last quarter of the nineteenth century saw the first stirrings of an interest in higher education for girls in England. Girls who were intended for the newly-founded schools for young ladies, like the Ladies College, Cheltenham, would certainly not find time for this traditional hobby for women. Rolled-paper work was very time-consuming, it was very messy for the fingers, and, in order to be successful, it required real artistic feeling in an age which was becoming increasingly scientific and utilitarian.

A good introduction to the technique of rolled-paper work is given by Hannah Robertson herself. "Filigree," she writes, "is a very pretty

Rolled-paper cabinet on stand. COURTESY LADY LEVER ART GALLERY, CHESHIRE, ENGLAND, with acknowledgments to the Trustees of The LADY LEVER ART GALLERY, PORT SUNLIGHT.

work, and when executed with judgement, will last hundreds of years and may be made to represent various figures such as beasts, birds, houses, flowers, trees, coats of arms, etc. The first thing proper to be done is to stain paper for these purposes with the various colours you chuse, such as green, done with Sap Green dissolved, yellow with gumbouge [gamboge] a vermillion colour, red with red, ink blue with liquid blue, purple with the purple colours in a receipt among the paints.

Rolled-paper and wax portrait of a sovereign, probably Queen Anne. COURTESY LONDON MUSEUM.

Rolled paper portrait of Queen Anne, incorporating a wax doll and an embroidered miniature picture. COURTESY VICTORIA AND ALBERT MUSEUM, LONDON.

"The best way to lay on the colours is to have your paper flat on a table and the paint laid on, and smoothed over with your hand; when dry, let it be glazed over; then deliver it to a book binder to be gilded and cut in very narrow slips, after which your own judgement, or a pattern, will direct you, whether you intend for picture or glass frames, boxes etc. Let the wood they are made of be fir, as the pins with which the rolled-up slips are fastened will not penetrate any other wood. Take care not to let any of the glue fall on your work after the filigree is laid on, because it will dim the gilding, and let the glue dry before you take it off the pins."

Amateurs who preferred a ready-made stained paper could buy it from the paper merchants, such as Abraham Price, at the Blue Paper Warehouse, in Aldermanbury, London, and Edward Butling of The Old Knave of Clubs at the Bridgefoot in Southwark, who were well-known paper stainers and gilders of the seventeenth century. Gilt and colored paper were also manufactured in Paris, and in other parts of the continent, such as Germany. The method used in gilding paper was a very simple one; any bookbinder, and quite a number of amateurs, could have carried it out. Slips of paper were pressed in a bookbinder's press, scraped flat, rubbed with red chalk or American bole, and glaired, that is, brushed with beaten-up white of egg. While the glair was still tacky, a sheet of gold leaf was lifted off the cushion on which it had rested and blown or laid onto the edges of the strips. When it had dried in place it was burnished with an agate, or a dog-tooth burnisher. Another bookbinder's technique ornamented rolled paper; the edges were not merely gilt, but tooled as well, with a cold or heated brass tool which made marks on the gold edge. Colored paper that has been gilt on the edge produces a magnificent effect, even after hundreds of years, during which the original color has faded to a shadow of its former self.

The paper spirals and rolls used were shaped and folded or rolled before they were applied to the picture as a whole. Usually the basic shape used was a coil or spiral, like a watch spring. In Austen's *Sense and Sensibility*, written in 1811, Elinor Dashwood helps Lucy Steel to make a filigree basket by offering to "roll the papers" for her. These rolls were probably immobilized while they dried by being pinned in place.

Whatever type of unit was used, the paper strips were always stuck down onto the composition with the gilded edge facing the spectator. Bands were used in which lunate-shaped pieces, consisting of three or four layers of curved gilt paper, alternated with a line of paper curled into a wavy line. Paper was rolled or folded in minute corrugations. It could be folded into square or diamond-shaped units. It could also be rolled in tight cones, or made into tassels, constructed or flattened rolls of paper, from the middle of which emerge waving fronds. All these devices were combined with the utmost ingenuity. A flower made from cones, for example, would be surrounded·by several outer rings of tightly rolled coils.

Sometimes the rolled-paper artist relied for her effects on just a few well spread out, tastefully arranged scrolls—as in the St. John in the London Museum. Filigree, however, was intended to consume a lot of time, like scrimshaw (whalebone carving). It is, therefore, not surprising that there seem to be fewer examples of bold scrolling, well spaced out, with many open spaces to let the white satin background show through, than there are of compositions in which the filigree is massed to cover every square half-inch. The most difficult of all rolled-paper work, building up three-dimensional figures, such as the heraldic beasts in the Victoria and Albert shield, was seldom attempted.

Many of the pieces which have survived must represent the work of a number of people working in cooperation, or of just one woman, whose task was a very lengthy one indeed. One heraldic shield contains about 6,000 pieces of rolled paper, just in the mantling of the crest alone. As some pieces of the mantle overlap others, the number of rolls and spirals may really be much greater. Like many other forms of art, rolled paper must have demanded not merely taste, but application, patience, and perseverance, even though, at this time, women's fingers were broken in to the task of rolling small pieces of paper in order to make curl papers for that other work of art, the curled locks that ladies of the period wore.

6
Mrs. Delany's Flower Mosaics

MARY Delany occupies a unique place in the history of paper art for several reasons. She is the best known of all English paper cutters. She owes this reputation not just to her talents, which were considerable, but also to her connections and friends. She was a close friend of George III, to whom she was always "dear Mrs. Delany." George, like his daughter, and other members of the English royal family, such as Queen Anne, was a keen amateur paper worker. Even before Mary Delany began the compositions for which she is famous, her "flower mosaics," she had charmed George with her rolled-paper pictures and paper models of temples. Mary Delany is also remarkable insofar as her works have survived entire and in good condition, if we discount the few early models which have already been mentioned. All too often we know of the work of paper artists only by repute because their work is the most fragile and evanescent of all art forms. Mrs. Delany had her flower mosaics bound up as she made them. They were religiously kept by her descendants, one of whom, Lady Llanover, presented them to the British Museum, London, where they can still be seen. The most extraordinary aspect of Mrs. Delany's work, however, is that she began making her mosaics at the age of 74, a time of life when failing eyesight has forced most artists to give up their work, or curtail it severely.

It is difficult to judge the flower mosaics she made objectively, because there is a glamor about the artist that continually intervenes between the observer and her works. Her contemporaries credited her with having invented the art form in which she worked. Would they have admired

Mary Delany. Pisum marinum, *Sea Pea.* COURTESY TRUSTEES OF THE BRITISH MUSEUM.

Mary Delany. Polyanthus Tuberosa, *Tuberose*. COURTESY TRUSTEES OF THE
BRITISH MUSEUM.

her so much if they knew that paper mosaics of flowers formed part of the stock-in-trade of the Turkish paper artist of the time? Probably they would, because there is a great deal of difference between eighteenth-century Turkish flower collage and Mrs. Delany's work. The Turkish collage artists made pictures of flowers; Mary Delany composed portraits of them.

Any reassessment of the flower mosaics demands some account of Mary Delany's life and the social circle in which she moved. Her friendship with George III enabled her to reproduce many exotic flowers that could be found nowhere in England except in the royal gardens at Kew, for example, some of the American flowers that she copied. Mary was herself, aware of this fact and when George III sent a flower to her to "paint" in paper she always made a note on the back of the composition that the royal gardener had supplied it from Kew.

George's admiration was probably just as necessary to Mary as his help. He had inherited from his ancestress, Mary Queen of Scots, a love of beauty and a talent for connoisseurship, just as he had inherited the fatal malady that estranged him from his American subjects. An artist can live more easily without patronage than without appreciation. Throughout her long and difficult task, Mary was sustained by George's respect for her work. In 1787, almost at the end of her life, a friend of hers, Mrs. Preston, commented on the close relationship that existed between her sovereign and Mary. "The King and Queen increase in affection and respect to Mrs. Delany, and the King always makes her lean on his arm. Her house is cheerful, and filled with her own charming works. No pictures have held their colours so well. I had time to look over near a volume of her flowers. She had finished nine hundred and eighty sheets, and regrets that the thousand she intended wants twenty of its full number."

One reason why the collection of flower mosaics that Mary had planned never reached its intended total of a thousand was the desire of members of George's family to acquire examples of her work. Queen Charlotte chose half-a-dozen flower compositions, including "Asparagus," one of the artist's most daring and successful flower mosaics, and Mary noted the spaces left blank in her album with the words "Selected by Queen Charlotte."

Like Augustin Edouart, Mary took up paper cutting to soothe the loneliness of a widowed life. Before she invented her flower mosaics however, she had been an enthusiast of various kinds of crafts. Possibly she had found in them a relief from a tragically spent youth. Mary Granville (as she was called before she married) had been born in May,

1700, the daughter of a very aristocratic family. Her father, Bernard Granville, the younger brother of George Granville, Lord Lansdowne, had arranged with her aunt, Ann, Lady Stanley, who was Maid of Honour to William III and Mary, that she, too, should stay at court and become a Maid of Honour. Queen Mary herself had put down her name on the waiting list of the Maids of Honour, but her uncle's political party, the Whigs, was defeated by the Tories, and this dashed her hopes of an appointment at court. Instead, she took up residence with her uncle, Lord Lansdowne, at his country seat at Longleat. There, her beauty, charm, and clever accomplishments brought a crowd of admirers to her. One of them was a young Mr. Twyford, with whom she fell very much in love. One rainy day, however, a rich Cornish landowner, a certain Alexander Pendarves, who was a friend of Lansdowne's, rode into Longleat to pay his respects to her uncle. Lord Lansdowne, she tells us, "was exceedingly pleased at his arrival and begged him to join them at once. I expected to have seen somebody with the appearance of a gentleman, when the poor, old dripping, almost drowned Gromio was brought into the room, like Hob out of the well. His wig, his coat, his dirty boots, his large, unwieldy person, and his crimson countenance, were all subjects of great mirth to me."

Unfortunately for Mary, her uncle did not share her poor opinion of Pendarves, who soon became a suitor for her hand in marriage. Lord Lansdowne could only see in his friend a rich and influential landowner who could swing several seats in Parliament to the Lansdowne interest. Mary was delivered up, a virgin sacrifice, to the political ambitions of her uncle. When her uncle threatened violence toward the man she loved, she gave in and unwillingly became, at seventeen, the bride of her sixty-year-old admirer. Twyford died shortly afterward—of a broken heart at the loss of his sweetheart, it was said—while Mary began a very unhappy married life with Pendarves. The borough-monger's first act, after marriage, had been to carry his bride off to Roscrow and immure her in a decaying castle which he owned there. The English country gentleman of the day was not without his good qualities, but Pendarves did not possess a single one of them. He ate and drank to excess, so much so that he usually came home drunk to bed. Heavy drinking gave him the gout, which made him extremely irritable, and to add to this irritability there was the fact that he was "furiously jealous," of his wife —without cause, it may be said. Mary knew her first happy moment in marriage when her husband died, leaving her almost penniless except for her jointure. Although without a fortune, she was still so beautiful that she did not lack for suitors. Lord Baltimore, Lord Tyrconnel, and

Mary Delany. Rubus odoratus, *sweet flowering raspberry*. COURTESY TRUS-
TEES OF THE BRITISH MUSEUM.

Mary Delany. Pyrus Cydonia, *quince*. COURTESY TRUSTEES OF THE BRITISH MUSEUM.

even John Wesley, who was very susceptible in his youth, came to court her. Her marriage had been so unfortunate, however, that she preferred not to risk matrimony a second time, but stay a widow, existing on a moderate income, but living a brilliant social life. Her greatest friend was Margaret Cavendish Harley, the Duchess of Portland, at whose country house at Bulstrode she was, much later in life, to create many of her most successful compositions. At her house in London, at St. James Place, near to the court at St. James Palace, she held her own little court of women writers, including Fanny Burney, Mrs. Montague, Mrs. Chapone, Mrs. Carter, Hannah More, and Mrs. Boscawen, along with dilettantes, artists and musicians, such as Horace Walpole, Dr. Burney, Handel, Garrick, and John Wesley, whose presence at her salon indicated her liking for men of religion as well as culture.

It was at the home of a cleric who was also a writer, Jonathan Swift, that she met her second husband, Dr. Delany, while she was on a visit to Ireland. Mrs. Delany was still alive when they met, so Mary's references to the doctor in her diary are confined to praises of his sermons. Some time afterward Dr. Delany became a widower; eighteen months later he proposed to Mary, and she consented. Patrick Delany was a man poor in fortune but rich in Irish charm and very much in love. Though the Lansdowne family felt that Lord Lansdowne's niece had made a mésalliance, Mary could take comfort in a husband very different from Alexander Pendarves. He was never tired of praising her sweet smile, her eyes, of which "he could never tell the colour, but to the best of my belief they are what Solomon calls 'dove's eyes.' She is almost the only woman I ever saw," he added, "whose lips are scarlet and bloom beyond expression."[1] Mary fought hard to get preferment for her husband, and succeeded. He was given the Deanery of Down. Mary and he moved into the Deanery of Down and there she painted a Madonna and Child for his chapel and made shell-flower work for its ceiling. For their villa at Delville, near Dublin, she designed marble inlay patterns for the floors of each room, which incorporated the device of a star, an allusion to Swift's "Stella." *Pietra dura* work of this sort may later have to her the techniques she was to employ in her paper mosaics. *In pietra dura,* the pieces of the picture fit into one another, just as the elements in a paper mosaic do. Both have an abrupt tonal quality. There is no fine shading; instead, the highlight of a fruit is silhouetted starkly against its dark background, and stares at the observer dramatically, like the pupil of an eye. In both *pietra dura* and flower mosaic, great effects

---

[1.] Quoted by Austin Dobson in "Dear Mrs. Delany," *Sidewalk Studies* (London: Oxford University Press, 1924), p. 119.

can be achieved by using the grain of the material.

Pietra dura, however, was only one of Mary's many accomplishments. She sculpted a portrait medallion of Esther Johnson, Swift's "Stella." She knotted in "sugar-plum" work, making covers and decorations for her homes. She embroidered beautifully, and "wrote a fine hand in the most masterly manner, and designed with amazing correctness and skill." Add to this the fact that she was an accomplished portraitist, who painted charming likenesses, such as that of her dear friend, the Duchess of Queensbury. Mary had been taught to draw by the famous painter, William Hogarth. She tells her sister, Anne, in a letter dated July 13th, 1731, "Hogarth has promised to give me some instructions about drawing that will be of great use—some rules of his own that he says will improve me more in a day than a year's learning in the common way."[2]

After fifteen happy years of marriage, her second husband died, and her great friend, "Peggy," Duchess of Portland, carried her off to Bulstrode, in Buckinghamshire, the Portland family seat, for a long visit, and ultimately persuaded her to make her home there during the summer months. It was at Bulstrode that a new chapter of her life opened with the invention of her "flower mosaic work." Now 74, Mary found her eyesight was failing and she was faced with the prospect of having to give up her beloved needlework, painting, and drawing. Tenacity ran in her family, however; one of her ancestors, Sir Richard Granville, had, with one ship, *The Revenge*, fought an action against fifty-three Spanish galleons and left many of them shattered hulks before he fell mortally wounded on his quarter deck. She was determined not to give up her artistic pursuits completely. Quite by accident, she hit on a new medium—new to everyone else in England as well as to herself—which she could still pursue, even with impaired eyesight.

"Having a piece of Chinese paper on the table of bright scarlet," she wrote, "a geranium of a similar colour caught my eye, and taking my scissors, I amused myself by cutting out each petal, by my eye, in the paper resembling its hue. I laid the paper petals on a black ground and was so pleased with the effect that I proceeded to cut out the calyx, stalks, and leaves, in shades of green, and pasted them down." At this point Peggy came into the room, and, mistaking the paper picture of a flower for the original, asked, "What are you doing with that geranium?" Her work immediately became enhanced in her own opinion by the fact that "my dear Duchess Dowager of Portland look'd on it with favourable eyes," and she determined to make some more flowers. "This paper

2. Ibid., p. 122.

mosaick," she writes, almost apologetically, "was first begun in the seventy fourth year of my age, which I at first only meant as an imitation of an *Hortus Siccus* [a botanical collection of dried flowers pressed in an album] as an employment and amusement to supply the loss of those that had formerly been delightful to me, but had lost their power of pleasing, being deprived of that Friend, whose partial approbation, was my Pride, and had stamp't a value on them."[3]

Artists are not always precise about the dates of their own work, and it has been pointed out that the seventy-fourth year of Mary's age, 1774, cannot be accepted as the real starting date for her first flower piece. The collection she left includes a *Rudbeckia laciniata* and two varieties of China aster dated 1773. These have been taken to be trial specimens because the background is shiny black paper, which is far less effective than the matt black paper that Mary almost invariably uses, and much of the flowers has been touched up with a paint brush. Altogether, the pieces made before 1774 may be looked on as experiments made while she was feeling her way toward her real medium.

In 1774 Mary only succeeded in finishing two flowers; in 1775 she made sixteen, in 1776 she made 160, and thereafter her output remained high. In 1782 she was forced by a further deterioration of her eyesight to lay her work aside, when she was only twenty short of the target of a thousand flowers which she had set herself. As she herself wrote:

> The time has come I can no more,
> The vegetable world explore,
> No more with rapture cull each flower
> That paints the mead or twines the bower . . .
> Farewell to all those friendly Powers,
> That blest my solitary Hours.

Encouraged by Peggy, who had plucked for her the treasures of the ducal parterres at Bulstrode, and by George III, who "took delight in these flowers," and ordered Opie to paint a portrait of the artist for his private cabinet, Mary had created a portrait gallery which included all the favorite English flowers, and many exotics. Even to look at the huge tomes which contain her delicate paper cuts, ranged in order in the British Museum in which are housed the books and maps of her old friend George III, one sees evidence of her untiring industry. She was indeed an indefatigable worker, and there are several references to her flower mosaics in her letters. In one she says: "I could write on, but must break off now as a flower awaits me." In another letter, dated

---

[3.] Bernard and Therle Hughes, Article in *Country Life* (January 25, 1952).

Mary Delany. Rubus fruticosus. COURTESY TRUSTEES OF THE BRITISH MUSEUM.

November 1780, and written from Bulstrode to Mrs. Francis Hamilton, she describes how she was "sitting at work at my paper mosaic in my working dress, and all my papers littered about me, when the groom of the chambers announced the Queen and the Princess Royal." Even when George III came to breakfast at Bulstrode she was not too excited to finish a cactus on which she was working.

The experiments which have been already mentioned had cleared the way for what may be described as her classic technique in carrying out

Mary Delany. Poincan pulcherrima, *Barbados flowerful.* COURTESY TRUSTEES OF THE BRITISH MUSEUM.

Mary Delany. Rosa canina, *Dog Rose.* COURTESY TRUSTEES OF THE BRITISH MUSEUM.

the new medium she had invented. Once she had adopted this method, she boasted that her only tools were scissors and paste, and her only material paper. To begin, however, she used a paintbrush and color as well. To take one example out of many, in *Amaranthus Tricolor*, the edges of the leaves are clearly indicated by paint. Occasionally, as in the case of one of her most successful compositions, the "Horse Chestnut," the flowers, as well as the ribs of the leaves, are painted.

One of her contemporaries, Gilpin, describes how she set to work, though his words must be accepted with some reservation. "In the progress of her work she pulls the flower to pieces, and having cut the shape of the several parts, she puts them together, giving them a richness and consistence, by laying one piece over another, and often a transparent piece over part of a shade which softens it. Very rarely she gives any colour with a brush." Though Mary may have taken a flower to pieces now and again, just to examine the shape of the petals, if she had done this continually before she picked up the scissors, she would have spoiled the silhouette of the flower, the aspect that she was most keen to seize.

Her classic method was as follows. She began by obtaining a freshly gathered or still growing plant. Often she picked these flowers for herself. Like Peggy, whom she describes as "a great lover of botany and well acquainted with all English plants," Mary knew her flora. In a letter of 1758 she describes herself as wandering among the herbs and flowers of the Dublin Mountains, and noticing in particular, "a little pale purple aster, with yellow thrum, that grows by lakes and near the sea." Sometimes the flower would have been sent to her as a present, such as one of the last which she copied, on 9th August 1782, a specimen of *Portlandia grandiflora* (named after her beloved Peggy), which George III had ordered the royal gardener to send her from Kew.

Having selected her subject, she placed it in a pot or in a vase against a sheet of black paper and folded in the middle so it stood upright. The black paper formed a foil for the brilliant colors of the flower, accentuating its highlights and shadows, and throwing the outline of the leaves and flowers into relief. Mary next cut out with her scissors every petal of the flower as it appeared to her. She made no preliminary sketches and only used her eye as a guide. The petals were then pasted onto a sheet of black paper, after which the highlights and darker parts of the blossom were put in by snippets of paper that were cut out separately. Flowers of one color, especially white ones, had to be made up in several different shades of the same color so that they would appear natural. "To produce this handsome, full-bodied cabbage rose," says Mrs. Edmund Gosse, "Mrs. Delany must have required no fewer than five tints of scolloped pink tissue-paper."[4] Lastly, the lights and shades on the bloom were stuck down onto their respective petals. Occasionally Mary would contrive a highlight, or a shade, by cutting out part of a petal, so that the color underneath showed through. She did this in her composition of the "Burnet Rose." Once all the blossom had been completed, the stamens, stem and leaves were cut out. When a petal or part of a petal was superimposed on a leaf, it was added last.

Mary was able to contrive an incredible number of shades of green to be worked into just one flower stem. She cleverly copied the technique of the *pietra dura* artist and used texture and grain to achieve some of her best effects. She would use papers of the same general color, but lay a smooth green paper next to one with a rough surface. She also employed the watermarked lines running across her papers very skillfully. The lines of the black background sheet on which the whole flower was pasted always ran from the top of the composition downward. These lines, almost invisible to the naked eye, formed a sort of internal frame for the picture by bisecting the lateral axis of the flower. The watermark on the colored paper used for the leaves was also used to build up the picture. Either it ran all in one direction so that it led the viewer's eye into the composition, or it branched off in different directions along the main rib of the leaves, so as to suggest the thrust with which they left the plant, each at a different angle.

The comparison between flower mosaic and *pietra dura* work must not be pressed too far. Mary achieved effects in paper that could not be obtained, or which could not be consistently obtained, in gem stones. Leaves boldly snipped out with a few slashes of the scissors are contrasted with the most minute and delicate tracery, such as the stamens of a horse chestnut flower. The folding of one leaf or petal over another produced gradations between the pieces of paper,which, though minute, are quite perceptible. Unlike *pietra dura* work, which is quite flat, flower mosaic seems almost modeled in relief. The combination of flat modeling and the matt black background makes the composition appear to swim away into space.

In some compositions dried leaves have been substituted for paper ones. Although Chalmers, in his *Biographical Dictionary*, tells us that Mary did this as a joke, and expected that no one would detect the substitution of a real for a factitious leaf, dried leaves are easily detectable, because they have a dull, lifeless appearance compared with the paper ones. It seems, on the whole, more likely that these leaves are the work of some injudicious restorer.

4. Mrs. Edmund Gosse, "Paper Flowers," *Temple Bar* (December 1897).

Mary Delany. Ranunculus ficaria, *Pileworth*. COURTESY TRUSTEES OF THE BRITISH MUSEUM.

Mary Delany. Rhodendron Ponticum, *Purple flowered rose bay*. COURTESY TRUSTEES OF THE BRITISH MUSEUM.

"Mrs. Delany was fortunate in the shades of colour of her papers," remarks Mrs. Edmund Gosse. "The greens are vivid and varied, without being ever crude, or arsenical, while her selection of yellows and pinks is a most happy one."[5] Mary's work was dependent for most of its effect on the color of the paper she used. The passing of the years has undoubtedly faded some of her colors, but one can still admire the brilliance of many of her compositions. Her early work as a rolled-paper artist had probably given her experience in staining her own papers. Some of the papers she uses seem to have been marbled by sprinkling them with small drops of water, or perhaps leaving them out in the rain.

When she did not make up her paper for herself she would take the greatest care to obtain just the tint which she required. "She used to procure various coloured papers from captains of vessels coming from China, and from paper stainers, from whom she used to buy pieces of paper in which the colours had run, and produced extraordinary and unusual tints. In this manner she procured her material, and was enabled to produce the utmost brilliancy where it was required with the greatest harmony of colouring from the various semitones of tint laid on."

Mary was a meticulous artist, a portraitist of the flower in miniature. The very delicate nature of her cutting is shown, for instance, on the prickles on the leaves of the Musk Thistle, or the hairs on the stem of the Burnet Rose. She approached her work with great seriousness. She usually signed every composition with a monogram, cut from paper, and pasted in the left hand corner of the picture. Sometimes this monogram was red; once it was lilac, when she was portraying a lilac flower. But in her later years, when she felt her eyesight failing, it was always in white, because, as she said: "I fancied myself nearly working in my winding sheet." Since Mary's compositions never left her home—except for a few royal commands—there was no reason why she should sign them at all, except for the fact that she was obviously working, not just for her own amusement, but for posterity.

Another sign of the importance which she herself attached to these compositions is the careful documentation which frequently accompanies them. She often notes the place where they were made, as well as the date on which they were finished. When, for example, she had finished that American flower, the *Tetrandia Monogynia*, she wrote on the back of the mount: "Made Bulstrode, 17 September 1778." Occasionally the notes are much more informative: "Finished Thursday, September 7th, 1781. The day after I had the honour of paying my duty at the Queen's

---

5. Ibid.

Mary Delany. Papaver rheus, *poppy.* COURTESY TRUSTEES OF THE BRITISH
MUSEUM.

Mary Delany. Potentilla recta, *cinquefoil.* COURTESY TRUSTEES OF THE BRIT-
ISH MUSEUM.

Lodge at Windsor." "Bulstrode, August 7th, 1778. Finished the day after the King and Queen were at Bulstrode." The composition that most marks her own consciousness of the need for precise information in assessing an artist's work is the *Saxifraga Stolonifera*. Underneath this blossom she carefully wrote out the Chinese name, in Chinese characters, followed by an alphabetical transliteration, and a translation. "*So Fo Yee*—Old Tyger's Ear. The Name written by Whang a at Tong, The Chinaman as he called himself." his note would seem to suggest that Mary had shown her picture to a Chinese visitor to England, and he had identified it, without any trouble, and given her the Chinese name of the bloom. The accuracy of Mary's power as a portraitist of flowers— to which she drew attention in this note—was borne out by Sir Joseph Banks, a scientist who accompanied Cook on his voyage to the Pacific. Banks used to say that Mary's flower pieces were the only pictures he had ever seen from which he could venture to describe botanically any plant without the least fear of committing an error. Though lifelike, Mary's flowers escape the lifelessness of a plate from a textbook on botany, partly because the impressionistic nature of the medium she used helps to avoid an excessive realism.

Mary seems to have left no record of what she herself regarded as her most successful pictures, and critics are divided on this subject. "She was most successful," writes Mrs. Edmund Gosse, "with the simpler and more humble of her sitters, such as the tiny white blossoms that sparkle in the grass." I personally would prefer those flowers which provided her with the greatest challenge and which produced bold *tours de force*, such as the Horse Chestnut, which was criticized by Mrs. Gosse as: "a rather messy production, with unintentional gum seeming to ooze from the petals."[6]

Mary certainly loved all her flower pieces as though they were the children she had been deprived of. Nothing less than the compulsion of a royal command from Queen Charlotte could have made her part with any of them, though after the death of Peggy she seems to have been quite poor, and had to accept a house in Windsor, along with a pension of £300 a year, as a present from George III. At Windsor she spent the last years of her life, visited by the royal family including that fellow artist in paper, Princess Elizabeth, and little Princess Amelia, whose "dear Lany," she was. She kept her sight till the last and must often have looked through her albums of flower compositions, which were a sort of diary of the happy days she had spent with Peggy at Bulstrode,

6. Ibid.

at St. James' Place, and in her little house at Windsor, and in some verses she inserted in her albums, she took a farewell of flower portraiture for ever:

> Hail to the happy Hours! When Fancy led
> My Pensive Mind this flowry Path to tread
> And gave me Emulation to presume,
> With timid art, to trace fair Nature's bloom,
> To view with awe the great Creator's Power,
> That shine confessed in the minutest Flower.[7]

7. Mrs. Delany's Flower Mosaics, Print Room, British Museum, London.

7

The Silhouette

THERE is nothing so American, throughout the whole range of paper art, as the silhouette. Although the silhouette is a very old idea and evolved from the cutouts in hide or bark made by primitive peoples, the paper profile reached the height of its popularity just as America was emerging as an independent nation. Major André cut a silhouette of Benjamin Franklin; Washington had his profile—a gift to the silhouettist—taken many times. Scarcely had the new republic grown to maturity than Augustin Edouart arrived as a visiting silhouettist to perpetuate the profiles of all the most prominent Americans of the time. Hubard, a boy genius, who, like Edouart, came to America from England, became a naturalized subject of the new country and died in the service of the Confederacy. Native American profilists vied with their foreign rivals during the nineteenth century. Though gifted with genius, the Americans lacked the imported glamor of their European rivals, and they never obtained as many patrons as Edouart or Hubard. They did, however, consolidate the silhouette as an art form which persists in America to our own day.

It seems almost incorrect to speak of silhouettes before the rise of the man who gave his name to this art form—Etienne de Silhouette, Louis XV's Minister of Finances. It is better to refer to these profile cutouts in black paper as shades, by which term, along with that of shadows, they were known in English-speaking countries before Augustin Edouart made their French name familiar.

The American painter, Benjamin West, accounted for the birth of the silhouette in ancient Greece in this famous historical painting. PHOTOGRAPH BY STELLA MAYES REED.

The shade cut from paper would appear to be an English invention. The first known profilist was Mrs. Elizabeth Pyburg, an artist of the end of the seventeenth century. Around 1699 Mrs. Pyburg is credited with having cut the first profiles associated with any well-known person, shades of King William and Queen Mary of England. The seventeenth century was an age of experiment in new media. Talented shell carvers cut out profile figures of their sitters in mother of pearl and filled in the details with engraving. The paper template required to shape the mother of pearl would itself be a ready-made shade of the sitter. The shapes for elaborate silk mosaics would also be silhouettes in everything except the name. It is, therefore, perhaps no accident that silhouettes seem to have been first cut in silk as well as in paper.

The first literary allusion to the shade or silhouette is made by Jonathan Swift, the great Irish satirist who was a close friend of Mary

Delany's beloved Patrick Delany. Writing some time before 1742, when the madness from which he suffered left him alone and silent in the hands of his keepers, Swift described how:

> To fair Lady Betty, Dan sat for his Picture,
> And defy'd her to draw him so oft as he piqu'd her
> He knew she'd no Pencil or Colouring by her,
> And therefore he thought he might safely defy her.
> "Come sit," says my Lady, then whips up her Scissar,
> And cut out his Coxcomb in Silk in a Trice Sir.[1]

Swift further tells us that the features of the sitter might be put in with a pin, or with embroidery, (a precursor of the embossing which Jane Eliza Cook was to use with such good effect), that pasteboard might be used as well as silk for the portrait, and that the finished profile was mounted on paper, and the likeness framed.

From England the shade passed to France, where, around 1750, these *portraits en ombre* (portraits in shadow) became the rage. The amateurs of the shade included the French statesman Etienne de Silhouette, a patriot who had made a deep study of the English financial system, lately in the capable hands of Robert Walpole, and who wished to introduce some of its rationalizations and economies to France, where the finances were in a terrible state of confusion. Silhouette began his economy campaign in 1759, but his well-meant efforts were laughed to scorn as the parsimony of a cheese-paring bureaucrat. Overnight, anything which seemed to have been made meanly or incompletely from overcoats without braiding and trousers without pockets to drawings in outline only, were christened *à la silhouette*. Poor Silhouette could not survive the ridicule poured on him. He fell from office, retired to his estates, and spent the rest of his life as a recluse, devoted to religion.

Several potent factors combined to give the silhouette a wave of popularity which continued until the beginning of the nineteenth century. One of them was the arrival, in Paris, of the *ombres chinoises*, or "Chinese Shadows," which appeared at least as early as 1767.

The Chinese, from whom this shadow-play entertainment was derived, had long had a juvenile theater that portrayed folk plays which were eagerly watched by young and old alike in the dusky streets of towns and villages throughout the Empire. The shadow play had passed to Java—where the plays given by Wayang figures are still the best known of all shadow theaters—to Siam, Persia, Turkey, and Egypt. All these figures depended for their effect on being made from transparent hide.

---

[1] *Miscellanies by Dr. Swift,* Vol. 13 (London: R. Dodsley, 1751), p. 198.

Silhouette of Benjamin Franklin, cut by Major André.

The figures of Mameluke knights, ships, castles, infantrymen, and cameleers, discovered in the Nile valley by Dr. Paul Kahle, had all been cut from leather specially prepared in India.

Transparent hide could not be made in Europe; it was a purely Asiatic technique, so when the puppet theater jumped from Turkey to Italy, its adapters toned down the plays (Karagioz, the great Turkish folk hero, had been portrayed with an enormous phallus) and it substituted black cardboard figures for hide-figures which became moving silhouettes.

In 1772 the most famous of all French shadow play producers, Séraphin, set up his shadow play at Versailles. It instantly became immensely popular, and Marie Antoinette arranged for three special shows a week to be given during Carnival, beating down Séarphin's asking price of 1,200 francs to 300 francs. Séarphin gave an all- family show which never showed anything scandalous or naughty. Even abbés could attend the *ombres chinoises* wearing their cassocks without creating a scandal. Everyone enjoyed Séraphin's plays—except a Russian visitor who walked out in the middle of a play in which a Russian wife complains that her husband does not beat her any longer, and therefore cannot love her, and is only reconciled with her spouse when he confesses that he has mislaid his stick. Visitors who thronged to Séraphin's theater, or to that of his English rival, Philip Astley, at 22 Picadilly, London, must have come away feeling they wanted a souvenir of the moving shadows in the form of a silhouette or a paper cut, just as visitors to the London theater in the following century acquired theater prints and ornamented them with tinsel to remind themselves of actors' roles that they had enjoyed.

Not only amusement, but science as well now became enlisted on the side of the silhouette, in the person of Johann Casper Lavater, a Swiss clergyman from Zurich, who had founded a school of physiognomy. Lavater believed that a man's character was stamped on his face—a comforting belief if you had the approved kind of features. Like most eighteenth-century authors, Lavater published by subscription. He accepted money, in advance, from his patrons, and sent them the book after it was published. As he prepared the subscription list of his *Essays On Physiognomy*, Lavater told his prospective readers that the silhouette was the best guide to a person's character, because it showed up the contours of the head better than any picture. "He that despises shades," he wrote, "despises physiognomy. The Silhouette is the justest and most faithful type of portraiture, when the light has been placed at a proper distance, when the shade is drawn upon a perfectly smooth surface, and the face placed in a position perfectly parallel to the surface. It is faithful, for it is the immediate impress of nature, and bears a character of originality, which the most dextrous artist could not hit to the same degree of perfection in a drawing from the hand."

Lavater does not seem to have told any of his intended subscribers that their silhouettes were useless for the purpose of his book. Instead, he rather hinted, once he accepted a silhouette from a subscriber, that it would certainly figure in *Essays On Physiognomy*. When the book finally appeared in 1794, it contained many silhouette portraits (though not as many as had been submitted). It also contained instructions on how to take a silhouette. The subject was placed by the profilist in a special chair, with a candle on a stand to his right. The candle threw his shadow onto a transparent screen on the right of the chair. On the other side of the screen the silhouettist traced out, on a sheet of semi-transparent, oiled paper, the lines of the sitter's face.

Silhouettes of this sort might be faithful delineations of shadows, but they were anything but faithful portraits of sitters. An element of exaggeration, almost of caricature, was required to seize a likeness. The mechanically-designed silhouette involved securing the sitter's presence in a special chair, expensive to acquire and cumbrous to carry around. The finished life-size silhouette was too large to be acceptable as a portrait. To make it small enough to frame, it needed to be reduced by a pantograph.

Some silhouettists, such as the American, Moses Chapman (1782-1821), were content to trundle their machines "universally allowed by

Eighteenth-century silhouettes of Hogarth (left) who taught Mrs. Delany how to draw, and Garrick. PHOTOGRAPH BY STELLA MAYES REED.

the best judges to be more correct than ever before invented," round Massachusetts, or even frontier America. More and more must have sighed for a simpler method. More and more sitters, on the other hand, must have wished, when they looked at their machine-made profiles, that they could have something more artistic.

Many silhouettists took, with relief, to scissors and card, instead of the cumbersome profile machine. Scissors could be used anywhere. The portraiturist could sketch his sitter in his home, or he could make a lightning cut of an aristocrat as he mounted the steps of the scaffold to the guillotine. Down to the present day, scissors and paper has continued to be the most popular method of making silhouettes, especially when they are made by amateurs.

Professional artists, on the other hand, were not satisfied with the simple black profile. They adopted new ways of wooing the fickle taste of the public. Shades were painted on card, ivory, porcelain, *verre eglomisé* (a glass with a gold or silver foil backing), or on convex glass which threw a portrait of the subject onto the background as a shadow profile. Painted silhouettes are beautiful. A portrait by Miers or Mrs. Beetham reveals delicate and diaphanous details, such as wisps of hair or muslin caps, which seem breathed onto the background. But these

compositions, beautiful though they are, have stepped outside the boundaries of the silhouette proper. They try to portrait details which would
not appear in the simple shadow of the sitter cast by the lights of his
home interior—that familiar domestic shadow which rendered the silhouette instantly recognizable to the sitter's family and friends. Some
silhouettists went even further. They abandoned black and white as
well as the simple outline, and profiles became miniatures, save for the
fact that the face was left black, because all the costume was painted
in color, even to minute accessories, such as jewelry. Other workers in
profile adopted the unsatisfactory compromise of picking out the details
of costume and hair style wtih gold, or bronze, on the black. The old,
natural effect of the silhouette was lost.

Like all other paper crafts, cutting silhouettes was considered to be
an eminently suitable pastime for young ladies. A textbook, written by
B. Anne Townshend, in 1816, laid down rules for cutting silhouettes
in the schoolroom, as well as for making paper cuts. "In the Art of
Cutting Out," Miss Townshend wrote, "It is difficult to render assistance
to the young artist by instruction, but a few rules may afford improvement by being observed. The paper calculated for the purpose is thin
black paper, either black or shining, according to taste; the scissors to
have long shanks, and short and sharp points. It is best to cut on the
white side of the paper, in order to distinguish clearer. When a group
of figures are to be cut, after designing the subject in the mind, cut the
general outline in a rough manner, and correct and finish them afterwards; flowers, on the contrary, must be carefully and exactly cut at
first; the fibres and open parts to be done after the leaves and blossoms
are formed. It is necessary to begin at the feet and proceed at the back
of the figure; attention must be paid, that the right and left arms are
both introduced and properly used, as mistakes frequently arise from
cutting on the white side of the black paper which gives an awkwardness
to the figure. Let the lines flow, as in drawing, according to the line of
beauty; straight and acute lines give a formality. Flowers should be cut
elegantly and careless; all twining plants are best adapted for the scissors.
Neatness and exactness must be particularly observed in cutting vases,
tablestands, etc. By drawing the designs first it takes greatly from the
merit of cutting, therefore, it is advisable for the learner not to begin
with doing so, but form the figures with the scissors without the aid of
the pencil. A figure which looks well in drawing has a contrary effect
in cutting; for in paper there must be more left to imagination; and it is
impossible to describe foreshortening with the scissors as with the pencil;

therefore the figures must be selected with judgement, so as to display the whole form."[2]

The silhouettes which Anne Townshend used to illustrate her book are certainly no argument for skill as a teacher. They consist of lumpy classical figures (one with a very unclassical-looking book and umbrella) decorated with an infill of white line, which may represent slash cutting, or gold or bronze lining. Fortunately she introduces a little light relief in the shape of a rustic merry making, and a scene of French chefs cooking frogs with garlic.

Miss Townshend was careful to give instructions both for silhouette cutting and paper cuts. She emphasizes in her preface that "every style of cutting is introduced that may be useful to those who wish to learn the art."[3] Many paper cutters agreed with her in refusing to confine themselves just to the silhouette. Even silhouettists of genius, such as George III's daughter, Elizabeth, found relief from the black shade in turning to paper cutting as an agreeable change. Elizabeth made silhouettes of her father, George, in full length, showing him wearing court costume. Though those profiles, like the likenesses she cut of her mother, Queen Charlotte, are delightful, she is at her best in cutting groups of children playing and scenes of cupids.

The blue morocco bijou scrap book with a silver lock and clasp in which she kept her cuttings was the solace of her long period of spinsterhood. During the Napoleonic wars, a suitable bridegroom for the Princess could not be found. All the young royal princes abroad had either lost their thrones or were dancing attendance at Napoleon's court. At forty-seven, however, which was a very mature age for a bride in those days, Elizabeth married the Landgrave of Hesse Homburg. Like Mary Delany, Elizabeth found happiness late in life, with a husband who inspired such devotion in her that she mortgaged part of her personal fortune to pay his debts.

In spite of its competitors, which included colored silhouettes, silhouettes lined with gold and bronze, red profiles (with all the details painted in black line, which cast a silhouette shadow on the background, behind the thick glass on which they were painted), and silhouettes painted on *verre eglomisé*, the plain black shade continued to delight many.

In the early nineteenth century it passed into the hands of a silhouettist

---

[2] B. Ann Townshend, *The Art of Cutting Out Designs in Black Paper* (London: 1815).
[3] Ibid.

Augustin Edouart, cutting out a portrait of Liston, an actor. PHOTOGRAPH
BY STELLA MAYES REED.

of genius, Augustin Edouart (1789-1861). Edouart was born in Dun-
kirk; he served in the army of Napoleon, became established in occupied
Holland, and lost his fortune there in 1813, when Napoleon was defeated
by the allies. The Napoleonic wars had been fought by England against
Napoleon, and not against the French, for whom there was no national
animosity. Edouart decided to try his luck in England, confident of the
same welcome that many of his fellow countrymen had already found
there. He arrived with a five-pound note and a medal he had won as his

sole possessions. After an unsuccessful attempt to teach French, in a market overstocked with native French teachers, Edouart took up hair work, and embroidered pictures in hair. After ten years of hair work, his eyesight began to fail, his wife died, and he fell into a deep depression. One evening, while in company with some young lady friends, his companions showed him some silhouettes which had been cut by a patent machine. Edouart said he could see nothing artistic about them, whereupon the girls challenged him to do any better himself. Piqued by their teasing, Edouart tore off a piece of an old letter, snatched up a pair of embroidery scissors, and snipped out a likeness of the father of the young ladies, which he then blackened with soot rubbed off a pair of candle snuffers.

The profile was so astonishingly good that his friends urged him to become a professional silhouettist. Edouart hesitated for a long time. At first, as he says: "I rejected the proposal with scorn and retorted that I would not profess a shilling business, that I would not expose myself to be pointed out as a black Profile taker, and by those means be cut from Society."[4]

Though he found it impossible to continue with hair work, it had been a gentlemanly art, the sort of craft that young ladies were eager to leran. Silhouettes were much more of a popular art. Edouart finally decided that it might be a good idea "to perform in public to divert the gloom from a sinking mind." He salved his artistic conscience by deciding that his silhouettes would be different from all the others being turned out by catchpenny performers. He would "make an art of what had been so long considered a mere mechanical process." He was going to limit himself just to the shade. "Profiles with gold hair on them," he wrote, "coral earrings, blue necklaces, white frills, green dresses, are ridiculous; the representation of a shade can only be executed by an outline."[5]

Determined, he went into training for his new profession. He limited the amount of wine, or even the number of cups of tea or coffee, that he drank each day, to keep his hand steady. He fought to grasp the essential personal element in every sitter so that he could transmit it into a black shade. At every sitting he would try to analyze what the salient parts of the likeness were. The position of the hand, the line of the forehead, and the angle that it made with the nose were all very important. So, too, was any personal habit, such as that of keeping one's

4. Augustin Edouart, *Life*.
5. Ibid.

Silhouette of Paganini, by Edouart. The musician's profile has been mounted on one of the special lithographed backgrounds that this profilist used.
PHOTOGRAPH BY STELLA MAYES REED.

mouth half-open, instead of completely shut. Edouart never flattered, but his silhouettes delighted his sitters by their truth.

Although his very first client, the Bishop of Bangor, was so pleased with his profile that he ordered forty copies to send to his friends, some of Edouart's most important clients were not the fashionable folk who thronged his studio, which he set up in Bath in 1826, but well-known characters of the Spa, such as beggars and doll sellers, whose figures were as much part of the Bath landscape as the Pump Room, and whose shades were eagerly bought as souvenirs by the visitors who came to take the waters.

Edouart cut out a portrait with snips of the scissors alone, without any preliminary drawing. He held his scissors between his thumb and the second finger after an accident had made his index finger stiff for a time. Every portrait he made was carefully duplicated, pasted in an album, and annotated, so that he could send copies on request.

Edouart never forgot, however, that he had been a soldier and a gentleman before want forced him to become an artist. No patron might obtain a copy of a silhouette of a lady patron without her permission. He even went so far as to chain and padlock the albums in which he kept his silhouettes in case any amorous sitter tried to steal a portrait of his beloved.

Though he was always extolling the virtues of the simple black shade, Edouart departed from his principles sufficiently to pose his full-length silhouettes against stock backgrounds, lithographed on a sheet of paper, which depicted a terrace with a view onto a picturesque landscape, or a drawing room opening onto the beach. Often a figure would be given a miniature lithographed copy of *The Times*, a sheet of music, or a letter to hold.

From Bath, Edouart moved around England and Scotland, stopping temporarily in Spas like Cheltenham, or University towns such as Edinburgh, where he made portraits of the court of the French King in exile, Charles X. Everywhere he stopped, he had a trade card printed. That for Oxford, England advertises:

> Likenesses In Profile
> Executed by Monsieur Edouart.

> Who begs to observe that his Likenesses are produced by the Scissors alone, and are preferable to any taken by Machines, inasmuch as by the above method, the expression of the Passions, and peculiarities of character, are brought into action, in a style which has not hitherto been attempted by any other Artist.
> Numerous Proof Specimens may be seen at the house lately occupied by Mr. Trinder, at the bottom of the High Street, Oxford.

Silhouette of Dr. Batherst, Bishop of Norwich, by Augustin Edouart. PHOTO-
GRAPH BY STELLA MAYES REED.

Two Bath characters, a fruit seller and a match vendor. Cut by Augustin Edouart in 1827. PHOTOGRAPH BY STELLA MAYES REED.

	S.	D.
Full Length	5	6
Ditto, Children under 8 years of age	5	6
Profile Bust	2	0
Duplicates of the Cuttings to any quantity, are for each,		
Full Length	3	0
Ditto, children	2	6

Attendance abroad, double, if not more than two Full Length Likeness are taken. Any additional Cutting, as Instrument, Table, etc. are to be paid accordingly.

No silhouettist was ever half so successful as Edouart at getting the great and wealthy to sit for him. He specialized in making profiles of whole groups of persons, such as the London Stock Exchange. But artistic success did not really compensate him for the wounds to his self-esteem inflicted by the general public, who pointed him out as "a man who does common black shades."[6] Landladies refused to lodge him. Passersby wondered when ladies accepted his arm and asked aloud, "Who can she be, that lady with the black shade man?"[7] The governor of a castle, to whom he had written to introduce himself, welcomed him warmly, until he found that he had misread Edouart's handwriting. He had taken him to be not a "profilist," but a "pugilist."

It may have been a desire to breathe a more democratic air, as well as to find new patrons, which made Edouart decide to emigrate to America. "The Americans," a friend had written to him, "are known to encourage talent of every description."[8]

Between 1839 and 1849 Edouart took the profiles of thousands of American citizens, including six presidents. The portraits of Franklin Pierce, John Tyler, William Henry Harrison, and John Quincy Adams are particularly striking. Other important sitters of Edouart's included members of Congress, senators, justices, jurists, generals, professors, clergymen, editors, and actors. He also portrayed many humbler Americans, including Red Indians, for whom he had a penchant, and slaves, who were often included in a family group at the request of their owners.

Edouart began his travels in America in New York, and he visited Saratoga, Boston, and Philadelphia during the first year of his stay. In 1840 he made a stay in Washington, returning later to New York before going on to Saratoga Springs. The Springs, like those of Bath, provided him with many patrons, whom he would meet as he wandered round the grounds, helping the ladies propel the hand car that took them round the Circular Railway to Congress Spring, taking his constitutional to Flat Rock Springs with the other gentlemen, talking politics with them in the Hotel gardens after dinner, or sitting in a rocking chair on the Piazza chatting with the other guests.

In 1841 Edouart traveled around the eastern seaboard and the South. Subsequent years until 1844, after which records of his journeys become scanty, were spent as a resident at New York, Boston, or Philadelphia, or in further travels. In 1849 the silhouettist sailed back to England on the *Oneida*, only to suffer shipwreck on the rocks of Vazon Bay off the island of Guernsey. Edouart himself was saved, but most of his vast collection of silhouettes went to the bottom of the sea. His albums had contained the duplicate silhouettes he made by doubling the thickness of the black paper from which he cut the profiles. The double paper

6. Ibid.
7. Ibid.
8. Ibid.

enabled him to make a firmer cut, and provided him with a pattern for future silhouettes of the same sitter. His duplicates were also a record of this life's work. They contained the meticulous notes about his subjects, where they lived, what their names were, when he had cut their shades, who their relatives were, even the names of the pets that they sometimes brought with them to the sitting. Now his life's work had perished in the shipwreck. Brokenhearted, Edouart presented what remained of his silhouettes to a Guernsey family who had given him hospitality when he became a castaway. He abandoned his art and retired to his native France, where he died some twelve years later.

Critic's opinions will always be divided about the merit of the work of Edouart's only serious rival, William James Hubard (1807-1862). His life was much too romantic to admit of sober assessment—it reads like a sketch for a novel by Charles Dickens.

It is in the Dickens country, in Chatham, that Hubard first became prominent. A gifted boy whose ancestors included the German sculptor Reinhardt, Hubard began his artistic career by snipping out profiles of the parson and the clerk during the services in church. An enterprising showman called Smith persuaded the Hubards to sell their son to him. William accompanied his new master to Ramsgate, where he opened the "Hubard Gallery" in September 1822. Smith gave out the "infant prodigy's" age as less than it really was, but he had no need to lie about the boy's talent. Hubard's work interested the Duchess of Kent, who was staying at Townley Hall, near Ramsgate. Like so many members of the English royal family, she seems to have been enthusiastic about paper crafts, and she suggested that the boy should move his studio to London, near to Kensington Palace, where she lived with her daughter, Princess Victorine, who was later to become Queen Victoria. Hubard refused the offer, though he did cut profiles of the Duchess and her daughter.

From Ramsgate, the Hubard Gallery moved on to other British towns, accompanied by a blaze of publicity, of which an advertisement in a Norwich paper of 1832 may serve as an example:

> Extraordinary Development of Juvenile Genius. Just arrived at Mr. Critchley's, cutter, Market Place, Norwich.[9]

> MASTER HUBARD the celebrated little artist, who by a mere glance at the face! and with a pair of common scissors!! not by the help of any machine, nor from any sketch by Pen, Pencil, or Crayon, but from sight alone!!! cuts out the most spirited and striking Likenesses in One Minute

9. Desmond Coke, *Silhouettes.*

—Horses, Dogs, Carriages, in short every object in Nature and Art are the almost instantaneous productions of his TALISMANIC SCISSORS.

At the end of his British tour, in August 1824, Smith and his protegé arrived in New York. Hubard went on show, together with "The Panharmicon, a wonderful piece of mechanism which performs a delightful concert of 206 instruments." All through his American tour, as the gallery moved from New York to Philadelphia, and from there to Boston, Hubard had to put up with the frustration of being billed alongside other attractions, such as freaks or the mummified head of an Indian chief. Finally, in 1843, he decided that he was too old to continue as an infant prodigy. If he wanted to fulfill his ambition to become a painter of portraits in oils, he would have to cut loose now. He broke with Smith, securing a substantial share of the profits of the gallery, and leaving a successor, Master Hawkes, in his place. Thereafter he only returned to silhouettes when, on a return visit to Europe, he cut shades for his board and lodging on his travels. By 1841 he and his wife, one of the Tabbs of Virginia, had settled down in Richmond. Deciding to augment his earnings as a portrait painter by making bronze replicas of the Houdon statue of George Washington, Hubard set up a foundry in Sidney, a suburb of Richmond. With the coming of the War Between the States, he switched the production of the foundry over from artistic bronzes to the Brook Gun, a weapon intended for the Confederate army. On February 12, 1862 he was blown up by a mortar shell which he was filling at the foundry.

Some critics, such as the great collector Desmond Coke, have condemned Hubard as a child prodigy who never grew up. His many admirers, on the other hand, find in his work a sure touch for a likeness, an impeccable rendering of animals' profiles and faultless embellishments with gold, bronze, or color—those extras against which his rival, Edouart, railed so bitterly.

Some of the magic of the silhouette disappeared with the passing of these two great nineteenth-century masters. At the same time, a new invention appeared which killed some of the appeal of the silhouette as a sentimental likeness carried by lovers—the daguerreotype. Although lovers had commented, "Oh, Hubard, thy scissors to nature were true,"[10] as they looked at the silhouettes of their mistresses, a silhouette of a young girl tends to resemble other persons besides the sitter, because of the prevailing fashions in hairdressing and dress. Not so a photograph; the day of the black shade was done.

10. Ibid.

In the best of times, the living gained by profilists had been scanty. Martin Griffing, an American silhouettist who had been crippled by a fall from a steeple, had been forced to travel the roads of Vermont and New York State constantly, just to get a pittance. J. Dempsey, a British profilist of the 1830s, charged only a shilling for the profile, which included frame and glass.

Faced with competition from the camera, many profilists gave up their calling in despair rather than struggle on. Martin Griffing found he could support himself more easily by making shoes than silhouettes; Hubard gave up silhouettes for painting and sculpture. William Henry Brown (1808-1883) an American profilist, gave up his art twenty years before his death and took a job on the railroad. Another American profilist, William King, who flourished around 1805, and who has been hailed as one of the best silhouettists of his day, disappeared, leaving a note saying he had gone to drown himself. The scanty artistic remains of many American silhouettists show that their working lives were short, and the conditions for their art unfavorable.

The silhouette was becoming a mere seaside amusement. "I took it into my head the other day," wrote an Englishman of the 1820s, "to walk into a shop and suffer 'the machine,' as they call it, to be passed over my visage, and here I am quite black in the face, with a smart ebonized frame and an inner gilt edge, all for four shillings! What a depreciation of the fine arts, if indeed this can be said to belong to them!"

By the middle of the nineteenth century few people had any doubts about whether the silhouette belonged to fine art or not. Silhouettes were very cheap. J. Gapp, a famous English silhouettist, who advertised himself as "the original Profilist for cutting accurate Likenesses, attends daily at the Third Tower, in the centre of the Chain Pier, Brighton," charged only a half a crown for a full-length. Anyone could afford a silhouette, and, because they were cheap and were produced at lightning speed by the profilists, they were disregarded. The cheapness of the silhouette, which Lavater had noticed as a virtue, had now become a defect.

All through Victoria's reign the status of the silhouette fell. As a girl the Queen had been cut by Hubard, as a young monarch she had commissioned a silhouette from Pearce. No European monarch after Napoleon III, who was cut by Pearce's son in 1858, appears to have commissioned a portrait silhouette. By 1896 S. J. Housley could write: "The curious likenesses, in this irreverent age, have found their last resting place upon the walls of the bootroom, or even the floor of the attic."[11]

11. S.J. Housley, "Shadows of the Great," *Strand Magazine* (1896).

Lord Byron, by Mrs. Leigh Hunt. PHOTOGRAPH BY STELLA MAYES REED.

By the time Housley wrote, the silhouette had sunk to being a music hall attraction, depending for its interests on the speed with which an artist like Harry Edwin, of the "Wild West" in London, could cut silhouettes of any notables of the day, such as Gladstone or Robert Browning, who were called for by the audience.

If professional profilists became discouraged, silhouettists of genius were not wanting among the amateurs. Earlier in the century, Mrs. Leigh Hunt, wife of the writer, had produced hollowcut profiles of many of her husband's literary friends, including Byron and Keats. It is significant that because she did not identify the profiles as she cut them, most of them can no longer be assigned to particular individuals.

Jane Eliza Cook is the most sprightly and gifted of all nineteenth-century amateurs. One of her albums, which contains beautiful conversation pieces, has been preserved in the British Museum, London. The silhouettes are cut from white paper and embossed, from the back, with needles of various sizes and a blunt knife. Like most amateurs, Jane added verses as well as silhouettes to her collection, such as those which she wrote in 1874, entitled *Mammon versus Love*. Her silhouette book illustrations, such as those for the *Ingoldsby Legends*, and her classical subjects after Wedgewood put her very close to the best professional silhouettists.

Several revivals of the silhouette have been attempted. In June 1932 Herbert Leslie, Art Master at Brighton College, Sussex, England, held an exhibition at Brook Street Galleries, Bond St., London. Like many silhouettists, he made paper cuts as well, and his book *Silhouettes and Scissor Cutting*, remained a classic in the field until Professor Raymond Lister, now Presdient of the Royal Society of Miniature Artists in London, published *Silhouettes*, in 1953. Though not completely dead, the silhouette is struggling for existence, and is at present a mere "shadow of a shade."

The Punch and Judy Show. Silhouette by Eliza Jane Cook. Miss Cook was a very talented Victorian amateur who filled in the white outline of her silhouettes with a pointed stylus of some kind, probably the ivory point used by illuminators. COURTESY BRITISH MUSEUM. PHOTOGRAPH BY STELLA MAYES REED.

"I had a little husband, no bigger than my thumb/I set him on a quart pot, and there I bade him drum." Silhouette by Eliza Jane Cook. COURTESY BRITISH MUSEUM. PHOTOGRAPH BY STELLA MAYES REED.

Scissorcut by Hubert Leslie, 1922. PHOTOGRAPH BY STELLA MAYES REED.

Silhouette of George III, cut by his daughter, Princess Elizabeth. PHOTO-
GRAPH BY STELLA MAYES REED.

Silhouettes by Princess Elizabeth, daughter of George III. PHOTOGRAPH BY
STELLA MAYES REED.

Eighteenth-century silhouette of Gibbon. PHOTOGRAPH BY STELLA MAYES
REED.

Silhouette of Queen Victoria, executed at Kensington by Pearce the elder at the Queen's special command. PHOTOGRAPH BY STELLA MAYES REED.

Victorian silhouette made by a profilist at the "Royal Aquarium," West-
minster. The silhouettist has added features, such as details of dress, brush-
ing them in lightly with gold. PHOTOGRAPH BY STELLA MAYES REED.

8

Pinprick

LIKE many other aspects of paper art, the story of the pinprick picture is a little conjectural. Pinpricking can, however, be traced back to China in the time of the Sung Dynasty (960-1280 A.D.) when an official memorandum, quoted elsewhere in this book, makes mention of "perforated" tomb paper. It has been claimed that pinprick pictures were known, much earlier, in Japan.

It was not until the eighteenth century that the pinprick picture made its appearance in Europe. There are several European arts to which pinprick is closely allied, and from which it may have evolved. The most important is lacemaking. The foundation for a piece of handmade lace, such as that made in Honiton in Devonshire, England, from the seventeenth century onwards, was an arrangement of pins driven into a pin cushion, which formed a design. Around these pins linen thread was wound and twisted, until the fabric of the lace had been formed. The position of the pins was all-important. On them depended the shape of the lace pattern. If the lace worker wanted to reproduce a particular pattern, which she normally would, since lacemakers created stock items, she had to ensure that they went back into the pincushion in exactly the same way. To do this, she created a pinprick picture the first time she pushed in the pins, by laying a piece of paper on top of the pin cushion. If she wanted a copy of this picture—to give to a friend, for example—all she needed to do was to print from it by laying a piece of paper on top and rubbing it with cobbler's heel ball. The pinprick pictures which were the master copies for lace looked extremely attractive in their own

Seventeenth-century Indian Moghul master drawing. One of a set pricked through for making a dusted tracing. PHOTOGRAPH BY STELLA MAYES REED.

right, so much so that they may have inspired artists to begin work in this medium.

Other artists were employing pinprick pictures as master designs in the seventeenth century. The Persian and Indian Mughal court painters, the only Islamic artists of any note who succeeded in breaking through the taboo against Mohammedans representing living beings, kept by them master drawings from which they could reproduce exactly any scene they had once sketched. These master drawings were pricked along the main lines with a pin. To trace from them all that the artist needed to do was to lay them on a piece of paper and dust a little bistre or powered red chalk onto the master drawing. This colored dust would filter through the pinprick holes, leaving a faint, but visible outline of the drawing on the paper underneath. The master drawings were made on what is called "chicken skin," a very fine, thin, semitransparent paper. The artists carried these masters about with them in their sketch books. From them they could produce the background and accessory figures of a court painting, which centered around some prince or nobleman, and then paint in, in glowing, enamel-like colors, the scenes of ceremonies, love, war, or hunts in the jungle, in which their patrons delighted.

Another Moghul master drawing. PHOTOGRAPH BY STELLA MAYES REED.

By the end of the eighteenth century, war and trade had brought many English travelers to India. For a time these English visitors enthusiastically adopted much of the Indian way of life, including wearing Indian dress and forming collections of Indian art. Some of these pinpricked master drawings may have found their way to England in the luggage of returning nabobs.

Pinpricking also figured largely in the outlines worked out for embroidery patterns. The first English pinpricks, which began to appear about the end of the eighteenth century, were much associated with costumes. They were often described as "Piercing Costumes On Paper," and their themes were sometimes adapted from fashion prints.

By the reign of Louis XVI of France, pinprick had become a fashionable craze which vied with the silhouette. Devotional pictures of the Virgin and the Saints, sometimes with scalloped borders, and occasionally touched up with paint, or ornamented with flowered backgrounds, were a work regularly carried out in convents. Lay work sometimes took the form of pictures of the French Royal family, and costume scenes copied from the fashion magazines of the day.

Marie Antoinette became one of the many sovereigns to take to paper work when she was imprisoned in the Temple. She managed to correspond, secretly, with a friend, the Chevalier de Rougeville, by pricking holes in curl papers which she sent out of the prison to him, sending him information which might help him in arranging her escape.

By the early nineteenth century pinpricking was so popular that special needles, varying in size from very fine to coarse, mounted in wooden handles, could be bought in craft shops to carry it out. Special spiked wheels, called "roulettes," were used to enable many holes to be pricked in a short time. Andrew Tuer, the great American historian of art who did so much to revive interest in papercraft, remarks in his *Old Fashioned Children's Book*,: "For filling spaces, two or more wheels were mounted on an axle. Without such appliances the more ambitious and microscopically minute pinpricked patterns could not have been achieved."[1]

The Young Ladies' Book, By A Lady, published in 1829, described the method recommended for "Piercing Costumes On Paper:" "Turkish and other figures in oriental costume are produced by a combination of water colour painting for the features, with a series of small punctures made with needles of various size for the dresses . . . The face, hands, and feet being first drawn and coloured, the outlines and folds of the

---

[1.] Andrew Tuer *Old Fashioned Childrens' Book.*

American pinprick? This picture of a black mother and her two children was made around 1780. COURTESY VICTORIA AND ALBERT MUSEUM, LONDON.

An anonymous English pinprick picture from about 1830. COURTESY VIC-
TORIA AND ALBERT MUSEUM, LONDON.

drapery are marked with a tracing needle. The paper is then laid upon a piece of smooth cloth or a few sheets of blotting paper, and the punctures inserted in the folds of the dress from the front to the back of the paper. The drawing is then laid with its surface downwards, and the interior of the various outlines filled up with punctures made with a very fine needle from the back to the front of the paper. It sometimes affords a pleasant variety if the costumes be wholly or partly coloured, as it relieves the monotony of the white. Needles of different sizes should be used at discretion, and the whole of the background or body of the paper painted in some sober opaque colour to throw up the figure."[2]

Pictures were often outlined in fine pinwork from the front, and pricked through from the back with a thicker needle to suggest a three-dimensional effect. Massed needle jabs producd the effect of heavier and lighter shading. Handmade paper, made from rags, had to be used to stand up to the punishment making a pinprick picture entailed.

The whole effect of good pinpricking rather suggests *cloué*, a medium in which ivory or tortoise shell is figured with designs made by inserting tiny gold nails. The figures of pinprick pictures are often skillfully painted, suggesting that their creators probably excelled in other media as well. Some of the surviving examples seem, like tinsel pictures, to have been suggested by the performances of favorite actors or actresses.

Pinprick is the last paper craft to arrive in Europe; it is also the earliest to disappear. One reason for its decline was the production, by the ton, of pinpricked paper produced by the mechanical embossing machine, which laps, in a frothy tide, along the edges of every Victorian valentine.

[2.] A Lady, *The Young Lady's Book* (London: 1829).

9
Paper Sculpture

WHEN paper sculpture first made its rather belated appearance in
Europe, which it did at the end of the eighteenth century, its subjects were almost all marine. I feel that it is possible to explain
this preoccupation with the sea and ships in two ways; either these early
paper sculptures developed out of a seaman's craft, similar to the modeling of ships and seascapes in wood shavings, which is also eighteenth
century, and which is associated with French prisoner-of-war work, or
they derived from that very popular theme of the *canivet* artist, the ship.

Fortunately for the latter hypothesis, it is even possible to point to
a bridging piece, a work which combines the essentials of the *canivet*
with that of paper sculpture. This interesting composition was made by
no less a person than Queen Anne of England, who lived between 1664
and 1714. Anne cut this ship with a penknife, and gave it to one of her
courtiers, in whose family it was long preserved. The ship, a paper cut,
was mounted on a sea of rolling billows made up of many scalloped
pieces of paper, stuck down on one another, so as to give a three-
dimensional effect. Queen Anne's invention was enthusiastically taken
up by the school of paper sculptors that was active some fifty years after
her death. Instead of contenting themselves with a flat paper cut married
to a three-dimensional sea, they used the same technique of overlapping
paper strips pasted to one another to compose the whole picture, so that
ship, sea, and harbor details possessed a marked sculptural effect, and
often seemed carved out of light-colored limewood. The paper which

Anonymous paper sclupture of the eighteenth century, probably Italian.
COURTESY HANS SCHWARZ, THE ANTIQUE SHOP, GREENWICH, ENGLAND. PHO-
TOGRAPH BY STELLA MAYES REED.

was so painstakingly overlaid, strip by strip, was thick enough to have
been cambered by scoring it with a rounded tool, such as a sculptor's
boxwood modeling scraper. Fine details were built up by attaching
minute snippets and threads of paper. The whole sculpture pushed out
from the back of the shallow box frame, supported from the background
by struts which are probably made of cardboard. The sculptors wisely
used paint very sparingly to touch up the model here or there, or
eschewed it entirely. After all, a completely painted model might be
made from any substance other than paper, and part of the attraction
of a paper model is that it is a tour de force, a sculpture undertaken in
a very difficult medium. When first made, these paper sculptures must
have been brilliant in their pristine whiteness, and it is probable that
they were originally set against a contrasting background, of some color
such as pale blue. The fading of the paper accentuated their present-day
resemblance to limewood carvings.

Of the several artists at work in this medium at the end of the eighteenth century, the most important was the Englishman, Augustine

Paper ship sculpture by Augustine Walker of Rye Sussex, England, 1761. COURTESY NATIONAL MARITIME MUSEUM, LONDON.

Paper ship sculpture by Augustine Walker, 1763. COURTESY NATIONAL MARITIME MUSEUM, LONDON.

Walker. He signs himself "Augustine Walker *Invenit* "[designed]" at Rye in Sussex. "Obviously he was a literate person, and his use of the Latin word *"invenit,"* a technical term in use among artists, suggests that he may have been a professional artist.

Everything about a Walker sculpture is carried out in incredibly fine detail. Even the rivet holes on the hull are represented, together with the lining on the sails. The tiny sailors aboard th ships are dressed in the motley costume of the period, the checked shirt of one man being beautifully rendered. Nothing has been forgotten aboard this ship sclupture. The ship's trumpeter is blowing his instrument on the poop. Little details, which can only been seen by peering, such as the quarter figures, the ship's boat, or the spars stowed on the deck, are given as much importance as the main lines of the hull. The high finish of these sculptures suggest that they are part of a numerous series, but in fact I know of only two, one dated 1761 and the other 1763, both in the National Maritime Museum, Greenwich, England.

The work of A. Van Omeringh, a Dutch paper artist who flourished in the 1760s, is known to us from a harbor scene, dated 1764, preserved in the Art Gallery, Manchester, England, and another, similar scene, in National Maritime Museum. Van Omeringh's work is similar to Walker's. The technique which both artists employ is the same. The strips of paper are cut, scored on the back, and built up layer by layer in a *trompe*

Paper sculpture group by Van Omeringh. COURTESY NATIONAL MARITIME MUSEUM, LONDON.

d'oeil effect which is held forward from the back of the frame by supports. Van Omeringh has a real Dutch appreciation of the picturesque effect of a seascape. His works are the translation of Dutch marine paintings into paper. Walker, on the other hand, is more interested in his ships than in the effect of the marine view as a whole.

There were many other sculptors of talent at work in this medium. I reproduce the work of an anonymous paper artist who probably worked in Italy, but whose interest is still centered on the sea. It is only possible to refer, briefly, to other workers in sculpture. Mariano Andreu produced a fine "Cavalier." Unknown artists, probably amateurs, produced exquisite little groups, such as Darby and Joan sitting together, he in a highback chair smoking a churchwarden, she in crinoline and shawl, seated before her spinning wheel with a distaff in her hand. Another paper sculpture of the nineteenth century shows a milkmaid who wears a dress painted blue and an apron and bonnet, sitting on a stile with her milk pail beside her.

Toward the end of the eighteenth century, schoolteachers in Germany began to feel that they could turn to good educational account the interest their children felt in paper sculpture by instructing them how to make it on mathematical principles. Instead of measuring out their paper models by eye, children were taught how to mark out the paper for modeling with a compass, setsquare, and ruler. Rousseau, a *philosophe* who took a deep interest in education, as his book *Emile* shows, had insisted that children's hands, as well as their minds should be trained. B. H. Basche, one of the teachers at the seminary at Schnepfenthal, near Waterhausen in Saxe Gotha, was a firm believer in Rousseau's teachings. Paper crafts figured on the syllabus of the seminary, and Basche decided to write a textbook on the art.

His book attracted a great amount of attention. It was translated twice into English, the first time in 1824, when it was given the extraordinary title of *Papyro-Plastics*. The book's translator, Daniel Boileau, said that it was intended to teach children "the art of modelling in paper with ample directions to draw with a ruler and compass the flat paper figure of the object to be represented and afterwards to cut, fold, joint, and paint the same, so as to form a neat representation of the given object on a small scale.

"This ingenious art," Boileau continued "is calculated to introduce children to the most common and practical applications of geometry, in a way which occupies their hands, and thus enforces their attention, without any particular effort of their thinking powers. By a law of nature, our curiosity, in our earlier years, is preferably directed to palpable objects . . . Complete figures, by which both the senses of seeing and feeling are gratified, satisfy the infant mind better than bare outlines; and the study of mathematics is likely to be prosecuted with more ardour after young persons have previously amused themselves with converting quadrangles and parallelograms into tables, chairs, houses, churches, bridges and ships.

"But independently of the mathematical studies for which it prepares the youthful mind, Papyro plastics, or the art of modelling in paper, has the additional advantage of teaching manual dexterity, the knowledge of proportions, a taste for the arts of design and above all, of affording a salutary antidote to that listless indolence, that pernicious love of cards, or that rage of reading any book at random, which are unfortunately tolerated in many respectable families during the long winter evenings, and which are alike unfavourable to the comfort and to the best interests of young persons, and greatly tend to obstruct them on their road to duty and happiness."[1]

The young paper craftsman was told to equip himself with "a pair of compasses, a common brass ruler, and a ruler in the shape of a triangle." He was to cut the paper either with scissors or a penknife. If he used the latter, he must remember to put a small board of soft wood under the paper he was cutting, and to leave tabs by means of which the different pieces of the model could be stuck together. The sculpture would have its component parts fixed with glue, gum arabic, paste, or the gummed labels used for sealing envelopes. "But everything depends on the goodness of the paper," concludes Basche, "which must be strong, stiff, and very smooth. Music paper, or drawing paper, Bristol board of the middle size, is the best."

The type of paper sculpture which Basche initiated, or popularized, is sufficiently familiar to everyone because it still appears on the outside of many breakfast cereal packets. The sections were cut out, folded or bent into shape, and stuck together by gumming the projecting tags.

The models which Basche described are fairly simple ones. They include: dice, a chair, a table, a chest of drawers, a sentry box, a thatched house, a pigeon house, an inkstand, a stove, a small house with gable roof, an ancient tower, a boat, sledge, ship, and windmill. Though elementary, these models are ingeniously planned, and have a very artistic appearance, especially when painted. Many young people who began by making them must have turned to more advanced work when they grew up. The kind of compositions made by amateurs in paper is described

1. *Papyro-plastics*, trans. Daniel Boileau (London: 1824).

by the author of *The Young Lady's Book*, published in 1829: "Working in pasteboard," she says "is by no means restricted to trifling productions. Very elaborate and exquisitely finished architectural subjects, ingenious models of the most delicate works, grottoes, trees, etc., and even views on an extensive scale may be admirably executed in parchment or paper, either in a plain state, or coloured to imitate the objects represented. The attempt to describe the mode of constructing such a class of works would be fruitless; proficiency in this amusing, and we may venture to say instructive art, is only to be attained by practice, taste, and natural ingenuity."[2]

Throughout the nineteenth century, paper sculpture continued to be carried out, both in the nursery and the boudoir. In 1870 the *Girl's Own Toymaker* instructed British children in the art of making fans, model cottages, and ladies wearing crinolines.

If there was one type of paper sculpture that especially recommended itself to young ladies, and threatened to eclipse all the others, it was the art of making paper flowers. The *Young Lady's Book* gave directions for making "charade flowers," artificial flowers cut from a paper strip and bent around a wire stem, which was usually covered with silk or fabric. Though all sorts of other materials, such as cambric and velvet, were used for making artificial flowers, paper was the favorite, because it was cheaper than the others. From about 1830, beautiful paper flowers began to be imported from China, where they were made from "rice paper." This substance is not really a paper at all, but is the pith of the tree *fatsia papyrifera*, ingeniously sliced into very thin sheets. The Empress Carlotta, tragic queen of the ill-fated Maximilian of Mexico, once paid $151 for a bouquet of various flowers made of rice paper. Children as well as grown-ups made paper flowers. In Harriet Mozely's novel *The Fairy Bower*, which was published in 1866, there is a description of how the heroine, Grace Leslie, outstrips all her playmates in making a little garden bower of paper flowers for a pet parrot. Cassell's *House Guide for 1875*, gives instructions for making paper flowers of this sort.

The jury of the Great Exhibition of 1851 remarked on the popularity of this hobby among adults. It is, they said "an art practised by ladies, who having first acquired it as an accomplishment, subsequently devote their leisure to its pursuit."[3] In France, centers of professional flower-makers were to be found at Lyons, St. Quentin, and St. Etienne, while in Paris, specialists assembled the already-constructed flowers into bou-

[2.] Ibid.
[3.] A Lady, *The Young Lady's Book* (London: 1829).

quets. These were sometimes used as the centerpieces of Valentines, or mounted on white card and framed as a picture. Garlands of white roses, leaves, and buds were mounted on a turquoise-blue background and framed in a recessed, shallow wooden box under a glass shade.

Most of the paper sculpture made during the nineteenth century had been constructed for the amusement of the artists who made it. With the turn of the century, paper art began to take its place in the art exhibition and became an important part of shop-window decoration.

One of the most significant effects of the *wycinanki*, that cut-paper work good-luck symbol, incorporating devices such as trees, swastikas, wheels, triangles, crosses and spiders, which Polish peasants pasted to the whitewashed walls and ceilings of their cottages, had been to interest professional sculptors in Poland in paper as a medium for academy work. The real precursors of this school of art were the humble Polish peasants who, from the nineteenth century at least, had adorned their shrines and Christmas trees with paper flowers and little figurines. All that the academic sculptors had to do was to adapt their methods to their own requirements.

In 1918 Jan Juratowski, a pupil of the Fine Arts School in Warsaw, exhibited two large figures in paper, a peasant and a drummer. Other professional artists followed his example with figures in the round and bas-reliefs exhibited at the Academy of Art in Warsaw. A world shortage of materials after the First World War brought about a new interest in paper as a cheap and easily sculptable material. Antoni Wajwod, a Polish sculptor, became famous for the paper sculptures he displayed at the International Exposition in Paris in 1937, and his work in the Polish Pavilion at New York's World Fair in 1939. A whole school of sculptors derived their inspiration from Wajwod, including Erica Hanka Gorecka. Although professional paper sculpture was to include brilliant American and British artists, such as Arthur Sadler and Bruce Angrave, it always owed a great deal to Polish sculptors like Marya Werten and Tadeus Lipski.

Between the end of the Second World War and the discovery of polystyrene, paper sculpture constituted the highlight of the window display at any important store. The course given by Erica Hanka Gorecka at Cooper Union in 1942 and the teaching and example of Marya Werten helped to focus public attention on the new medium. Artists such as Jan Kepinski, Zygmunt Kowalewski, and S. Niczewski gave the general public an interest in paper art that they have never had before or since.

10

Collage

*H*ENRI III of France seems to have originated collage. He cut out
many of the miniatures of the saints from his books of devotion, so
that he could stick them onto the walls of his chapel. Jacques
Auguste de Thou was so struck by the king's hobby—a rather destructive one for the royal library of manuscripts—that he gave it some publicity in his *Universal History*. Kings find many imitators of their
pleasures; a century after Henri's death collage had become a mania in
France. Special prints were being produced just so that they could be
cut up, colored and stuck down on a foundation to constitute a kind of
assembled picture. Favorite subjects for collage prints included the
flourishes and headpieces to be found among printer's ornaments, cupids
with quivers, emblems of all sorts, musical instruments, angels, and
many others.

Nativity prints were cut up to supply the necessary landscape backgrounds for collage pictures. Before long, prints were being published
in which the figures stood out by themselves on a blank background,
figures which had been designed and printed, just so that they could be
cut up to make collage. In spite of their ephemeral nature, some of
these printed sheets of figures have survived. Particularly popular as
collage subjects were printed crèche figures, and saints. A whole group
of French printers and publishers worked from the seventeenth to the
nineteenth century producing sheets of figures for collage.

For those who did not have the patience or the skill to make collage
pictures for themselves, ready-made collage was available. At Strasbourg,

Joseph Ettinger decorated a whole series of Biblical scenes, Moralities, and Saints, which had been engraved in copper plate, then cut out, pasted to colored backgrounds, and ornamented with enrichments of gold and silver paper. These archaic-looking saints, decorated with tinsel and color, are the ancestors of the tinsel-print characters of nineteenth-century England.

Some publishers, such as Nicholas Langlois in Paris, and Jean Louis Daudet of Lyons, who were active at the end of the seventeenth century and the beginning of the eighteenth, did not confiine themselves to gilt paper and color in producing ornamental collage. They issued prints of saints, which had been cut out and ornamented with rich velvets and gilding, set against a background of red silk.

Not all French collage was intended just for pictures. The cutout figures were often stuck down on furniture that was afterwards lacquered. Boxes, reliquaries, and the backgrounds of crèches were also ornamented in this way. To meet the demand of the collage enthusiast who wished to use his compositions on furniture, Bresson de Maillard, a professional paper cutter of the Rue Saint Jacques, Paris, cut out images and designs just for this purpose. Ladies bought them to stick on screens, lamp shades, boxes, and furniture. Special prints began to appear destined to be cut up and used on furniture. These prints were almost always sent out hand-colored, and they were expensive. Like pictorial collage prints, they were produced in France, though many came from Italy and Germany as well. The subjects of the prints were pastoral, exotically foreign, and sometimes a little gallant. The figures in the prints, peasants, street performers, beaux and their ladies, usually stood on a little patch of ground which had to be cut out. Probably these collage figures, which might represent artistes like street musicians, or acrobats, and the backgrounds on which they were intended to be pasted—views of castles, forests or formal gardens—suggested to nineteenth-century England the Toy Theatre, a model theater in which figures were moved to and from the wings on wire sliders. These figures had been cut from a special print, or series of prints, embodying the whole cast of a drama, with the scenery and backgrounds. he figures were first cut from the paper, then colored, and finally stuck on a cardboard "actor" to give solidity. The sheets of characters could be bought plain, at the cost of a penny, or colored, for twopence—hence the expression, still heard nowadays, "Penny plain and tuppence coloured." The patrons of the juvenile drama, who were mostly children—although they probably included some stagestruck adults—usually preferred to buy plain sheets and color them for themselves. The toy theater was a very gripping amusement,

Model theater figures. These prints of King William IV of England and his Queen, Adelaide, have been colored, tinseled, and cut to the silhouette shapes required before being mounted on a stiff background so that they could be inserted in a toy theater. The publisher of this theater print, Skelt, has been immortalized by Robert Louis Stevenson in his essay on the model theater. COURTESY LONDON MUSEUM.

especially performed in the darkness of the drawing room, lit only by the tiny oil lamps which illuminated the stage. Unfortunately, some plays were too much like the real thing, such as a horrific drama, called *The Miller and His Men*. The stage directions for this piece called for colored fire when the mill went up in flames with the robber band. Not infrequently the model theater, and sometimes the drawing room, went up in flames as well. Toy theaters had appeared in 1811, the first notable publisher of theater sheets being William West. Some of West's plays were republished by a publisher known as J.K. Green, who in turn handed on his stock-in-trade to one Redington, and by 1876 Benjamin Pollock had begun publishing them. Until a year or so ago you could buy Pollock's play sheets for plays like *The Blind Boy*, and *The Brigand*, sheets full of the artistic and romantic flavor of Regency England, for just a shilling or so—but those days are gone, along with the shilling.

Closely allied to the model theater figure was the tinsel print. London theatergoers of the 1830s often commemorated their admiration for a

Tinsel print of an actor playing Richard III. 1830. COURTESY LONDON
MUSEUM.

Tinsel print of an actor. 1830. COURTESY LONDON MUSEUM.

favorite actress or actor by buying a print showing him performing in one of his most popular roles, such as a print of G. French acting as Harlequin, published by Redington. Next they colored the print with water color, and bought tinsel to decorate it. The tinsel took the form of gilt and colored paper shapes representing any number of accessories to an actor's costume: epaulets, helmets and crests, armor, jewelry, belts, necklaces, and so forth. There were over nineteen different varieties of swords alone that could be purchased for the stationers who supplied tinsel. These shapes were then stuck down on top of the colored figure to produce a collage picture. When framed in a bird's-eye maple picture frame, the tinsel print has a really striking effect. Like so many forms of paper art, tinsel-print making has died out completely.

It was unfortunate that the enthusiasts for collage, who filled the Paris of the eighteenth century, were not content to buy the specially printed borders made for collage enthusiasts, and fill them with figures and landscape taken from specialized collage prints. They often used whatever print came to hand, with the result that they destroyed many art treasures. Mademoiselle Aïssé, a beautiful Circassian girl who had made her home in France after a series of romantic adventures, and who was a friend of Voltaire, commented on the fashionable craze: "There is a rage at present among people of society to cut up coloured prints. Everyone does it, from the greatest in the land to the humblest. These cut outs are stuck to cardboard, then varnish is spread on top. Wall hangings, screens, and fans are made up in this way. There are books of prints which cost up to two hundred *livres*, and women who are mad enough to cut out prints costing a hundred *livres* apiece. If this goes on, they will be cutting up Raphael's prints next."[1]

Typical of the fashionable collage amateurs of the eighteenth century was Charles Dufresny, a poet who collaborated with the dramatist Régnard in writing plays. "He had," said his biographer, "no talent with the pencil, brush, or pen, but he had dispensed with the need for them by taking, from different prints, figures of men, animals, plants, or trees, which he cut out, and from which he composed a picture which he designed in his imagination only. He arranged them, and stuck them down, according to what he thought the subject demanded. Occasionally he even changed the expression of faces, which did not suit him, by getting rid of the eyes, mouth, nose, and other parts of the face, and replacing them by others, suitable to express the emotion which he wished to depict. So sure was he of the effect of the whole composition

---

[1] G. Magnien, *Canivets, Découpures and Silhouettes* (Lyons, 1947), p. 8.

Tinsel print of "Mrs. W. West as Elvira." 1830. COURTESY LONDON MUSEUM.

that he wanted. Surprisingly enough, this collection of pieces, taken up, apparently at random, and with no preliminary sketch, formed an agreeable whole."

In England, as well, professional collage artists were at work, such as Thomas Burkett, who in 1776 exhibited, at the Society of Artists, a coat of arms composed of 426 pieces of paper. Possibly Mary Delany, who creates her own very distinctive kind of collage, may have received the original inspiration for her work from seeing a piece of this sort, rather than from the Turkish collage, which in some ways resemble her "flower mosaics."

Tinsel print. "Mr. Elton as Richard Coeur De Lion." This theatrical print, published in 1831, has been first colored, then overlaid with prefabricated tinsel ornaments, of which a great variety were available. COURTESY LONDON MUSEUM.

The next important development of collage in England took the form of colored flower pieces, invented by an invalid lady called Amelia Blackburn, and called after her "Amelias." These collages are compositions of flowers, foliage, trees, birds, animals, and fish worked into a paper mosaic. The individual elements of this picture are so small as to be almost invisible to the naked eye. The heads of some flowers are no bigger than the head of a pin, yet all are painted and shaded so accurately that they blend in with the background and the whole composition appears at first sight to be a painting rather than a collage.

The parts of such pictures, such as the tiny feathers on a bird's wing, no thicker than a hair, are cut from ordinary white kitchen paper, hand-colored with water color and brush, and stuck down on a black background. Where it is necessary to emphasize any detail, pinprick is used.

The size of Amelias varies greatly. Wreaths of flowers, which may include roses, forget-me-nots, daisies, pansies, lilies of the valley, and tiny green leaves, may be no larger than four by six inches. Bird pieces tend to be a little bigger. The theme of Amelias is often an exotic, tropical scene of hummingbirds, or birds of paradise, among luxuriant foliage. Amelia Blackburn in some ways resembles Douanier Rousseau, the nineteenth-century French painter who reveled in jungle and desert scenes but never left France. The English collage artist likewise tried to compensate for her inability to travel by living in a far-off world of the imagination.

It would be difficult to find a greater contrast to Amelia Blackburn's collages than those of Johann Jacob Hauswirth. Hauswirth's work has some connections with the collage of other European countries—Poland, for example—but as I suggested before, it still has a very local flavor. The subjects for his pictures are all homegrown: the migration of the cows to their Alpine pastures in the summer, peasants feasting, and hunting parties. The migration of the herds, or *remuage*, as it is called in Switzerland, allows him to picture the beasts and their herdsmen slowly winding up the mountain tracks, so that there are two planes of action to be seen at once. Many figures cross the pictures in opposite directions. They form groups which are compartmentalized, but not separated. The collages are built up on a background of white paper on which gummed pieces of variegated, flowered, or printed paper, and are squared off with a gay border.

In Poland, collage and paper cutting began as peasant arts that were eventually to pass outside the boundaries of local folk art and inspire professional artists, first in Poland, then all over the world. I have coupled collage with paper cutting here because it is difficult to

Polish wycinanki. *Notice how related to modern collage this purely traditional vase of flowers is.* COURTESY HORNIMAN MUSEUM, LONDON.

Polish wycinanki *showing a village wedding.* COURTESY HORNIMAN MUSEUM, LONDON.

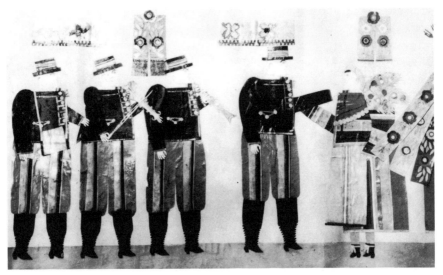

Another view of the wedding wycinanki. COURTESY HORNIMAN MUSEUM, LONDON.

draw the line between them in Poland. In one local center, Seiradz, for example, the characteristic paper ornament, or *wycinanki*, as it is called in Polish, was an eight-pointed star. Young girls cut out these stars in different colors and in diminishing sizes. Next they applied them, as collage, directly to the wall of a room, building up a composition piece by piece, each smaller star fitting inside another of a larger size and a contrasting color.

Wycinanki began as a religious decoration for the festivals of Easter and Christmas. They were cut from colored paper, folded, and twisted to give a symmetrical pattern. Sometimes these patterns were four-sided, sometimes multiple, so that a whole row of spruce trees might decorate the wall of a room. Altogether there are more varieties of *wycinanki* than any other kind of paper art form. Though Christian in purpose, Polish paper cuts may have been imitated from Jewish art, or from the Turkish Empire to which Poland formed a barrier for so long. Magical and pre-Christian motifs appeared in the *wycinanki*, symbols such as the spruce tree, representing the tree of life, and the arrowhead. Alongside these mystic good-luck symbols could be found Christian motifs such as the cross, the monstrance, and the cockerel, symbol of Easter. Other designs included squares, rectangles, and interlacing circles, animals and birds, and stylized scenes of peasant life, such as a village wedding.

The artist cut his, or rather I should say *her*, composition (because most *wycinanki* were made by young girls), purely by eye. There was no drawing out of the design on the paper first. The girl cutter used an ordinary knife or scissors, or occasionally the shears used for clipping off the fleece of a sheep.

So far as I have been able to discover, *wycinanki* are the origin of our present-day Christmas decorations. These paper ornaments were not only used at Christmas, as well as Easter, to decorate the joists of a room in the peasant's home, its windows, the newly whitewashed a walls, and the sacred pictures; they often took a form which we can still recognize in modern Christmas decorations. They had applied fringes that were apparently peculiar to Polish paper art; they were often arranged in bands or ribbands, and frequently shaped into circles, polygons, and stars. *Wycinanki* were also used all over the house, around the windows and so forth, just like modern Christmas decorations, at a time when contemporary Christmas decorations in America and England were confined to holly and ivy.

Wycinanki first appear in Poland about the middle of the nineteenth century, a time of comparative calm, and one during which a slight improvement in the lot of the peasantry took place that enabled them to spend more time on decorating their homes. The art of Polish paper cutting had arisen from magical good-luck symbols, formerly painted on the walls of Polish houses, and from decorations cut from leather or hide. The latter form of craft goes back a long way into Polish history. As late as the twentieth century cut-work designs were still being applied to the belts made in Cracow and the overcoats worn by mountain dwellers in various parts of the country. The designs which used to be applied to these belts and coats were now transferred to the paper decorations, where they fused with the old magical protective signs and with the purely Christian ones that heralded the coming of Easter and Christmas.

By the end of the nineteenth century, every district in Poland had developed its own regional type of paper cut. The patterns of these regional *wycinanki* were traditional, but they were by no means static, and they often changed to meet the demand for novelty. The many local variations in paper cuts can all be comprised in just three regional groups: Lowicz, Kurpie and Lubin. These town names are used, merely as a matter of convenience, to designate types of paper cuts which stretched far outside the immediate limits of the places concerned. The Lublin paper cut, for example, was common to the whole region between the Bug and the Vistula.

Wycinanki. COURTESY HORNIMAN MUSEUM, LONDON.

The Lowicz type of *wycinanki* was essentially pictorial. It represented groups of people working the fields, or attending a village marriage or baptism. Lowicz paper cuts were often made up of brightly colored pieces of paper, sometimes gilt or silvered, stuck together to produce the effect of a kaleidoscopic collage. Kurpie paper-cut artists drew their inspiration from the designs used for local woodcarving. They found no trouble in amalgamating purely Christian motifs, such as crosses and monstrances, with pagan ones, like the spruce tree. Horses stand beneath the symmetrically arranged branches of these trees, a trait that recalls the work of Johann Jacob Hauswirth. Tiny hares also enter into the paper cuts, while stars, made up of tiny, superimposed pieces of paper, are also characteristic of Kurpie work. The many-colored stars, just as much collage as cut-work, represent one side of Kurpie *wycinanki*. Plain, solid colored cuts represent another, and a third consists of realistic paper cuts of men, animals, and birds such as the Easter rooster, all collaged from multi-colored pieces of paper.

Merrymakers at the village wedding. Polish wycinanki. COURTESY HORNI-
MAN MUSEUM, LONDON.

Pattern for a four-fold Polish wycinanki. *A piece of paper is folded four
times; the design is cut out on it, then the paper is opened up. A beautiful
square symmetrical paper cut is produced.*

The Lublin style includes designs of trees with stylized branches, eight-
pointed stars, and strips of paper whose decoration recalls that used on
local embroidery patterns.

Polish paper cuts helped to popularize, if they did not originate, two
departures in twentieth-century paper art. The collages of peasant weddings were built up with several layers of paper, making the surface of
the composition bulge out, like a bas relief. Professional artists in Poland,

Twentieth-century Polish wycinanki, *in which cockerels, the symbols of Easter, peek at one another.*

inspired by three-dimensional paper cuts of this sort, and by the little Christmas-tree figurines, took the not very considerable step of creating academy paper sculpture. A Kurpie paper cut of 1909, in which the bulging figures bear faces cut from prints, and have tresses of real hair, brings us to the threshold of modern artistic collage—even though to the peasant creator it was merely a way of modifying an old theme to render it more attractive.

Today, Polish paper cuts have become somewhat divorced from their social background, a peasant class that liked to have nice possessions of their own, and their religious origin, a devoutly Catholic people welcoming the arrival of the church's greatest festival. Paper cuts of today are more likely to commemorate the Palace of Culture and Science in Warsaw than the coming of Easter. *Wycinanki* are to be found in executives' flats as well as in the whitewashed cottages of the farm laborer, and the hope of winning a prize in a state- sponsored exhibition has to some extent replaced the original spontaneous desire to beauty the home. Kurpie and Lowicz still remain important centers for *wycinanki*, and in areas of Poland where the art has died out in the past, such as Sieradz, it has now been revived.

Envoi

*U*NLIKE many other natural products, paper is still a raw material for much living art. Apart from the traditional pioneers of this art, forerunners with whom this book, as a history, has of necessity been obliged to concern itself, there are many modern sculptors and artists—too many to be mentioned by name, even briefly, here—who use paper as their principal medium. Since it is the world's youngest natural art material, it is to be hoped that the great days of art in paper lie ahead of us.

Bibliography

Anonymous. *Canivets De La Collection Gabriel Magnien*. Lyons: Lescuyers & fils.

Boileau, Daniel. *Papyro-plastics*. trans. London: 1824.

Braybrooke, Richard Lord, ed. *The Diary of Samuel Pepys*. London: Frederick Warne, 1887.

Cassells. *Book of Sports and Pastimes*.

Coke, Desmond. *Silhouettes*.

Mrs. Delany's Flower Mosaics. Print Room, British Museum. London.

Dobson, Austin. In "Dear Mrs. Delany." *Sidewalk Studies*. London: Oxford University Press, 1924.

Edouart, Augustin. *Life*.

Giles, Herbert A. *The Civilisation of China*. London: Williams and Norgate, 1911.

Gosse, Mrs. Edmund. "Paper Flowers." In *Temple Bar* (December 1897).

Housley, S. J. "Shadows of the Great." *Strand Magazine* (1896).

Howe, Bea. "Parlour Accomplishments." *Country Life* (December 10, 1948).

Hughes, Bernard. "English Filigree Paper Work." *Country Life* (September 21, 1951).

Long, Basil S. *Antiques* (February 1931).

Lady, A. *The Young Lady's Book*. London: 1829.

Magnien, G. *Canivets, Découpures and Silhouettes*. Lyons, 1947.

Jules, Michelet. *The Insect*. London: Nelson and Sons, 1875.

Mitford, A. B. *Tales of Old Japan*. London: Macmillan, 1883.

The Travels Of Marco Polo. London: Heron Books, No date.

Robertson, Hannah. *Life*. Birmingham: 1791.

Rubi, Christian. *Cut Paper Silhouettes and Stencils*. London: Kaye and Ward.

Shonagon, Sei. *The Pillow Book*. trans. Ivan Morris. London: Penguin Books, 1967.

Miscellanies by Dr. Swift. Vol. 13. London: R. Dodsley, 1751.

Townley, Lady Susan. *My Chinese Note Book* London: Methuen.

Townshend, B. Ann. *The Art of Cutting Out Designs in Black Paper*. London: 1815.

Tuer, Andrew. *Old Fashioned Children's Book*.

Index